THE GREAT ADVENTURE

STORYBOOK

A Walk Through the Catholic Bible

Emily Cavins, Lisa Bromschwig,
Regina Lickteig Neville, Linda Wandrei

Illustrated by: Eileen McCook

ASCENSION PRESS

West Chester, Pennsylvania

Ascension Press
Post Office Box 1990
West Chester, PA 19380
1-800-376-0520
AscensionPress.com

Cover design: Mike Fontecchio
Layout and design: Stella Ziegler
Illustrated by: Eileen McCook

Printed in the United States of America

ISBN 978-1-945179-10-5

Contents

Foreword

Children love stories. They never seem to grow tired of hearing them, even the same story told over and over again. Throughout their lives, they may hear individual stories from the Bible, but few will grow up understanding how these stories "fit in" with the whole. Without a complete understanding of God's plan for us as told in the Bible, they may end up with a disjointed and incomplete view of God and the Catholic Faith.

Growing up with a true understanding of who God is, who we are, and how we are called to live can be difficult in our current secular culture. Our children will no doubt encounter ideas that are very different from the story given to us in God's Word. This can confuse them and make them uncertain in the Faith. Part of our responsibility as parents and educators is to accurately convey God's Word to the next generation, teaching them to discern truth from falsehood.

In the sixth chapter of Deuteronomy, Moses tells the Israelites, *"These words which I command you this day shall be upon your heart; and you shall teach them diligently to your children, and shall talk of them when you sit in your house, and when you walk by the way, and when you lie down, and when you rise"* (Deuteronomy 6:6-7). If the people of Israel were to be faithful to God in a foreign land, they needed to teach their children his ways. So, too, must Catholic parents diligently teach the Faith to their children so they can remain faithful to God's ways in the midst of a secular world.

Jesus said, *"My sheep hear my voice, and I know them, and they follow me"* (John 10:27). Children come to know the voice of God by hearing it proclaimed in the Bible. The Word of God is like a seed that is planted in young hearts. As it grows, it will accomplish what God wills—a deeper relationship with him.

When children read the Bible with their parents, they are experiencing God's Word with those they trust the most. The Bible gives children wisdom for living, direction for their lives, and comfort in so many ways.

The foundation for everything we believe as Catholics springs from salvation history, the "big story" found in the Bible. If God's children do not know this amazing story, they will not understand their place within it. If a biblical foundation is not built in the hearts of our children, the sacramental life of the Church—especially the Liturgy—will not be seen in light of the whole story. What meaning is there in the Creed or the sacraments if their role in salvation history is not understood?

From reading the Bible, children will come to know the heart of their heavenly Father as well as his amazing deeds for us. In the Bible, they will find examples of how God has worked with people in the past. As they grow older, they will come to see that, since God is eternal and does not change, he can work with them in a similar way.

When we face difficult situations, we need to know that we can turn to God and trust in him. As the stories of the Bible become part of our children's lives, they will receive wisdom and counsel from God's Word and be able to articulate their faith to friends and family.

This *Great Adventure Storybook* presents the story of salvation in a way that engages kids' minds and hearts. As they read the *Storybook,* they will come to understand the Bible as a *story*—and learn how this story is fulfilled in Christ and his Church.

What better way to engage our children with Jesus than to read to them the best story ever told? Jesus wants each of his children to hear about his love: *"Let the children come to me, and do not hinder them; for to such belongs the kingdom of heaven"* (Matthew 19:14). We bring our children into the kingdom of God, the Church, through baptism and promise to raise them in the Faith. Taking time to read the Bible is an important way we can fulfill this promise.

In the course of reading the Bible together, parents and their children will not only learn salvation history, they will build a memorable relationship with one another rooted in a shared faith. This deepened knowledge of the Catholic Faith can be the subject of discussions at the dinner table, at family gatherings, on trips, etc.

If our desire is for our children to grow up and change the world—and if we want our children to teach their children—then we must begin now by reading the Bible with our sons and daughters, and bring them into the story. This simple exercise will prove to be some of the best time we have ever spent. So, seek to plant God's Word into the hearts of your children and pray that God will do amazing things in their lives.

Jeff Cavins, Creator and President,
The Great Adventure Catholic Bible Study Program

Acknowledgments

- To our husbands, **Jeff, Kurt, Tom,** and **Phil,** for their support and promotion

- To **our children,** who participated in our programs

- To the dedicated team at **Ascension Press,** who worked diligently in the development and publication of this revised version of the *Storybook*

- To all of the **families and churches** who assisted with the "testing" of the stories with their children

- To **Fr. Mark Dosh** for his reflective and clarifying edits

- To the **130 individuals** who assisted in funding the development and initial publication of this *Storybook*

Chapter One

Introduction:

Welcome to the Bible Story

What is the Bible?

The Bible is also called the Word of God or Sacred Scripture. The words in the Bible are **inspired** by God and tell of his loving plan for all people. The Bible is one of the most popular books sold all over the world. Actually, it is more than just a single book: It is a "library" of seventy-three books. God inspired human authors to write the books of the Bible (CCC 105–107). When we hear the Bible readings proclaimed at Mass or when we read the Bible ourselves, we hear God himself speaking to us.

Why do we study the Bible?

We study the Bible so we can know the plan of God for our lives and can experience his great love for each of us. In the pages of the Bible, we learn the story of our salvation, how God planned from the beginning of the world to send a Savior, Jesus, who would defeat sin and death and who would offer all people eternal life with God. The Bible is the guidebook for living as a Christian, so it is important to read and study it.

Who will help us understand the Bible?

We know that God used human beings to write his message. The Holy Spirit continues to help us today to understand what these writers from thousands of years ago have written. When we pray before reading the Bible, the Holy Spirit will guide us. The Church has given us the *Catechism of the Catholic Church* (CCC), which is a reference book for studying and understanding the Catholic Faith and reading the Bible within the context of the Church's history and Tradition. (Guidelines for interpreting Scripture can be found in the *Catechism* in paragraphs 101–119.)

How are the books of the Bible arranged?

The books in the Bible are divided into two sections, the Old Testament and the New Testament. A *testament* is a **covenant** or agreement. The Old Testament has forty-six books, and the New Testament, which tells about Jesus Christ and the Church, has twenty-seven books. The first four books of the New Testament are called *Gospels*, which means "good news." The Gospels are especially important because they tell us about the life of Jesus, and we give them special reverence by standing at Mass during the Gospel reading. Many think that the Bible can be read from beginning to end to get a complete picture of the overall story, but the Bible's books are not in chronological order. Rather, they are grouped into literary categories such as history, poetry, prophecy, and letters, making it difficult to find the narrative. The *Great Adventure Storybook* makes it easier to learn God's story by following the narrative (or "historical") books, which present the events of salvation history in the chronological order.

What is the basic story in the Bible?

The Bible as an entire collection of books is a true account of salvation history. The books of the Bible follow the lives of real people and tell their stories. Within the many stories found in the seventy-three books of the Bible, there is one amazing overall story. The Bible story tells how God created everything, including people, and that everything he created was good. Sometimes, though, people reject God by choosing to disobey him. This disobedience is called sin, which results in separation from God and, ultimately, death. God makes a way for people to come back to him through his Son, Jesus Christ, by Jesus' death on the Cross and his resurrection. In other words, God became man in order to free humanity from sin. When Jesus ascended into heaven after his resurrection, he sent the Holy Spirit to guide the Church as it continues his saving work. When we are baptized, we become part of the Church, so the story of the Bible is really a story that includes us! It is the best adventure story that anyone could ever imagine, and we are part of it. When we read the Bible, we learn that God loves us and that he wants us to share in his perfect love forever. As you read the *Great Adventure Storybook* along with the Bible, remember that the biblical heroes like Abraham, David, and the Blessed Virgin Mary are part of your story, too. You are part of their family.

How do I use the *Great Adventure Storybook* to help me learn the story?

This *Storybook* is a summary of the plan of salvation found in the Bible and is designed as a companion to Scripture. It follows God's amazing plan, story by story, and it is written to help you see the vital link between the Bible, the Mass, and the Catholic Faith. This *Storybook* includes a Bible Reading Checklist at the beginning of each chapter.

How to Use the
Bible Reading Checklist

The Bible Reading Checklist directs you to the portions of the Bible to be read for each chapter. After the checkbox, a Bible reference gives the name of the book, followed by the chapter in bold type and the verses in regular type. The verse or verses are listed after the colon (:). If only a portion of the verses within a chapter are to be read instead of the entire book, a hyphen is used.

Example:

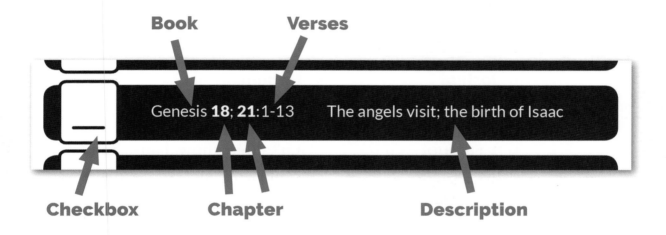

For the example above, read all of chapter 18, and in chapter 21, read only verses 1-13.

After reading from a particular Bible text, make an "X" in the checkbox and then read the summary portion in the *Great Adventure Storybook* that has the same title as the reading description.

Some reading selections are marked as optional. These are familiar Bible stories that provide additional points of view but are not necessary for the flow of the story.

The Narrative Books

The *Great Adventure Storybook* follows the story of salvation history based on twelve narrative books found in the Old Testament and two in the New Testament—the Gospel of Luke and the book of Acts. It also includes stories from other books of the Bible, known as *supplemental books*. Some supplemental books are noted in the Bible Reading Checklist for each chapter. The *Great Adventure Storybook* summarizes the narrative from the following books:

- **Genesis**
- **Exodus**
- **Numbers**
- **Joshua**
- **Judges**
- **1 Samuel**
- **2 Samuel**

- **1 Kings**
- **2 Kings**
- **Ezra**
- **Nehemiah**
- **1 Maccabees**
- **Luke (Matthew, Mark, John)**
- **Acts (Revelation)**

The Bible is God's gift to humanity. It includes a total of seventy-three books that tell the story of a variety of different people, places, themes, and subjects. This *Storybook* focuses on the fourteen books of the Bible that, when read in succession, give you the "who followed who" story of salvation. The other fifty-nine books, which we call the "supplemental" books, are listed on page 189.

The Time Periods
of the Bible Story

The *Great Adventure Storybook* separates the summaries into twelve periods of Bible history as seen in the chart below. A color-coded bar and icon appear in the outside margins of each page to indicate the corresponding time period.

SYMBOL	TIME PERIOD	NARRATIVE BOOKS
	Early World	Genesis 1–11
	Patriarchs	Genesis 12–50
	Egypt and the Exodus	Exodus
	Desert Wanderings	Numbers
	Conquest and Judges	Joshua, Judges
	Royal Kingdom	1–2 Samuel, 1 Kings 1–11
	Divided Kingdom	1 Kings 12–22, 2 Kings 1–17
	Exile	2 Kings 18–25
	Return	Ezra, Nehemiah
	Maccabean Revolt	1 Maccabees
	Messianic Fulfillment	Luke (Matthew, Mark, John)
	Church	Acts (Revelation)

Additional Features of the
Great Adventure Storybook

A circle indicates one of the six covenants God made with his people as found within the narrative books of the Bible. A *covenant* in the Bible is an agreement between God and one or more persons. Everyone involved in the covenant promises to do their part by agreeing to the terms of the covenant and by swearing an oath. (The six covenants are defined further in "The Six Covenants Established in the Bible" in the appendix on page 190.

Progression of the six covenants in the Bible:

 One Holy Couple: Adam and Eve (Genesis 1–3)

 One Holy Family: Noah and his family (Genesis 9)

 One Holy Tribe: Abraham (Genesis 15, 17, 22)

 One Holy Nation: Moses (Exodus 24, Deuteronomy 29)

 One Holy Kingdom: David (2 Samuel 7:11-15)

 One Holy Church: Jesus Christ (Matthew 16:18; Luke 22:1-23)

Conversation Starter Questions

At the end of each chapter, there are a few questions to help facilitate discussion of the chapter. These are only suggestions to help the reader personalize and internalize the story.

 A banner indicates portions of the Nicene Creed that coincide with the Bible. (A full reading of the Nicene Creed is in the appendix on page 193.)

 A cross indicates where in the Bible one of the seven sacraments finds its origin. (A listing of the sacraments is found in "The Seven Sacraments" in the appendix on page 194.)

 The rosary beads indicate one of the twenty mysteries of the Rosary when they occur in the Bible. (The twenty mysteries are listed in "Scriptural Origins of the Rosary" in the appendix on page 198.)

Bold italic text indicates that this Bible passage is used in Mass as one of the responses of the congregation. (All of the bold italic quotes are listed in "Scripture Quotes Used in Mass Responses" in the appendix on page 200.)

References Used in the Stories

- The **Catechism of the Catholic Church** (abbreviated CCC) is referenced in parentheses when a concept from the Bible is more fully developed in the *Catechism.*

- **Bible verses** that are not included in the Bible Reading Checklist of a particular chapter are also referenced in parentheses.

- **Terms** in **bold** are defined in the glossary beginning on page 180.

All Scripture is inspired by God and profitable
for teaching, for reproof, for correction,
and for training in righteousness …
                                    – 2 Timothy 3:16

So God created man in his own image;
male and female he created them.
– Genesis 1:27

Chapter Two

God Creates Our First Parents

Narrative Book: Genesis 1–11

Bible Reading Checklist

	Genesis **1**	The creation of the world
	Genesis **2**	The creation of Adam and Eve, the Sabbath, angels
	Genesis **3**	The fall of Adam and Eve; God plans to save his creation

Genesis 1
The Creation of the
World

Nicene Creed

I believe in one God, the Father almighty, maker of heaven and earth, of all things visible and invisible.

I believe in one Lord Jesus Christ, the Only Begotten Son of God, born of the Father before all ages. God from God, Light from Light, true God from true God, begotten, not made, consubstantial with the Father; through him all things were made.

God has always existed. This God is three equal Persons who share one divine nature. The Holy **Trinity,** the Father, Son, and Holy Spirit, had no beginning, has always existed, and will be forever (CCC 290–292). In his great creativity, God created time and he made our world from nothing (CCC 338).

The book of Genesis begins with two stories of Creation. Though different, they both show that everything God has created is good and that he loves what he has created—and he will always continue to nurture it. The first story (Genesis 1:1–2:9) describes Creation this way: *In the beginning, God created the heavens and the earth* (Genesis 1:1). God created the earth over a period of time, which the Bible calls the six days of Creation. On the first day, God separated light from darkness. On the second day, he made the sky. On the third day, he separated the land from the seas; and on the fourth day, God put the sun, the moon, and the stars in the sky. On the fifth day, he filled the seas with fish and the sky with birds. Finally, on the sixth day, God created all the land animals, and he created man in his own image and likeness, male and female. Each time God created something, he called it good, and when God created people, he said it was *very* good. God created everything, including you and me. He wants us to be here!

A carpenter uses hammers and nails to build things out of wood. A painter uses a canvas and paintbrush to create beautiful pictures. But God didn't need any tools or ingredients to make the heavens and the earth. God spoke the words, *"Let there be light"* (Genesis 1:3) and it happened. There was light. So God used his words to make the heavens and the earth (CCC 102; John 1:1). His Word is powerful!

Genesis 2

The Creation of
Adam and Eve

In the second Creation story (Genesis 2:10-25), after God created the
heavens and earth, he made the first human being—a man named
Adam. He formed Adam out of the dust of the earth and "breathed"
into him to make him come alive. Then he made a female partner
for Adam so that he wouldn't be alone. When Adam was fast asleep,
God took one of the ribs from Adam's side, and he formed the first
woman out of it. She was named Eve, and she became Adam's wife. God made
people to be more like him than anything else in the world. God made people
in his image. People are special to God because he gives each of us a soul living
inside us that will live forever. We are also special because we can know who God
is. We can love him and obey him. God gives people "free will," which means
people can choose whether or not to love and obey him (CCC 1704).

**Sacrament
of Marriage**

God Creates the
Sabbath

God worked for six days to create everything, and then on the seventh day he
rested. God wants us to rest one day a week also, which is called the
Sabbath. On that special day, we worship God and rest in his work.

God Creates
Angels

The Bible tells us that God made the angels, also called "hosts
of heaven" (CCC 326–327; Isaiah 45:12; Psalm 103:19-21; Luke
2:9-15). Angels are spirits who can talk to God and people. They
are special messengers who can go wherever God sends them,
from heaven to earth and back again. One angel decided that he

wanted to be greater than God. He wanted everyone to worship him instead of God. So he was cast out of heaven and came down to earth. That angel's name was Lucifer, and he is also called the devil, or Satan. He hates God and he tries to get people to do the wrong things. Satan also convinced some other angels to follow him, and they are called demons (2 Peter 2:4; 1 John 3:8; John 8:44; CCC 391–392). Demons are enemies who try to harm us by drawing us away from God, but we need not fear because God protects us and gives us the strength to resist temptation (Mark 1:27, 6:7; 1 John 4:4; CCC 447).

Genesis 3
The Fall of
Adam and Eve

God gave Adam and Eve a beautiful garden called Eden. God met with them and instructed them to take care of the Garden and the animals. He gave them the fruit of every tree to eat except one. He told them not to eat the fruit from a special tree, called the Tree of the Knowledge of Good and Evil.

Satan came into the Garden in the form of a serpent, a large, snake-like creature. The serpent came to Eve, and he tempted her with the lie that if she ate it, she would be like God. Eve took the fruit, tasted it, and gave it to Adam, who also ate it. After they ate the fruit, their eyes were opened and they felt ashamed. They realized they had disobeyed God and that they had "fallen" into sin. God called to them, but now they were afraid of him so they hid. Because of their disobedience, sin and death entered into the world. Their sin is called **original sin.**

God's Plan to
Save His Creation

God punished the serpent by making him crawl on his belly forever, and declared that one day a descendant of the woman will crush the serpent's head. This promise of God is the beginning of the good news that God will redeem people from sin. As for Adam and Eve, God gave them animal skins to wear so they would not be naked. God designed a way for male and female to work with him to create babies so that within a woman's **womb** new life can begin. This is how people can obey God's command to be fruitful and multiply. God also taught Adam how to grow food for them to eat. There was another important tree in the Garden of Eden called the Tree of Life. After Adam and Eve sinned, God did not want them to eat of the Tree of Life, because if they did, they would live forever knowing good and evil. As an act of mercy, God made them leave the Garden and put a fiery angel near the tree to guard it.

The good news is that God had a loving plan to help people to once again be able to live in his presence. God gave a promise (Genesis 3:15) to our first parents, Adam and Eve, that someday one of their descendants would defeat the Serpent, Satan. That descendant, as we will see in our story, is Jesus, the Savior of the world who conquers sin and death to bring us all back to God the Father who created each one of us.

Sabbath 7

What do you think?

1. How do you keep holy the Sabbath day?

2. In what ways are Adam and Eve like us, and in what ways are they different?

3. How do you know that God loves you by observing the world around you?

I establish my covenant with you,
... and never again shall there be
a flood to destroy the earth.
– Genesis 9:11

Chapter Three

God's Family Grows

Narrative Book: Genesis 1–11

Bible Reading Checklist

Genesis **4**	Cain and Abel
Genesis **6**	God asks Noah to build an ark
Genesis **7**	The Flood
Genesis **8**:1–**9**:17	God's covenant with Noah
Genesis **11**:1-9	The Tower of Babel

Cain and Abel

After Adam and Eve left the Garden of Eden, they had two sons, Cain and Abel. Cain, the older son, learned how to farm, and Abel, the younger, learned how to raise sheep and goats. God showed them how to bring sacrifices to the altar as a way to worship him. One day, Abel brought a sacrifice of his best animal to give to God as a way to thank God for all he had given to Abel. Abel sacrificed a lamb that was very dear to him. His brother, Cain, on the other hand, did not give God his best offering, nor did he have a thankful heart when he offered it. Therefore, God wasn't happy with Cain's offering. Cain became angry with God for liking Abel's offering more than his. Cain became so angry and envious of his brother that he killed Abel out in the field. As punishment for Cain's actions, God sent him to wander the earth away from the LORD's presence. Cain's sin separated him from God and other people. Eventually, Cain and his wife wandered to a new place and built a city there. Sadly, the people who came to live in it were very wild and did selfish things.

Adam and Eve did have more children, and one of their other sons was named Seth. He was a man who loved God and had many children and grandchildren. Seth's family followed God's ways and eventually one of his descendants, Lamech, had a son named Noah. Much later we will learn that Jesus also descended from Seth's family line.

Genesis 6
God Asks Noah to Build an Ark

The Bible tells us that Noah was the most righteous man on earth in his day. A righteous person is one who is good. Noah lived in a time when there was a lot of evil and violence in the world. God was disappointed in the bad choices that people were making. All of the people did bad things except for Noah, his wife, and their three sons and their wives. So God decided to send a flood to wash away the wickedness from the world. God told Noah to build a giant boat, called an ark, so Noah and his family could live in it while the rains flooded the earth. God also told Noah to take two of every kind of animal and bird onto the ark with him, so they could all stay safe and be protected from the waters of the flood. Then God sent the rain, and for forty days and nights, it poured!

Genesis 7

The Flood

The earth was flooded, and all those who had acted wickedly were washed away. The water remained on the earth for a time, but gradually the level went down until the ark settled on the top of a mountain called Ararat. Noah sent out a dove to fly over the earth, and it returned to Noah holding a small olive branch. This was a sign that Noah and his family could leave the ark and start new lives upon the earth.

The great Flood reminds us of our own baptism because the water washes away the wickedness from original sin and offers a new beginning of goodness. The ark reminds us of the Church, where we can live in faithful obedience to God and know that he will protect us.

God's Covenant
with Noah

After Noah, his family, and the animals came out of the ark, they built an altar and made a sacrifice of birds to God. God placed a rainbow in the sky as a sign of a covenant, or promise, that he would never again flood the whole earth.

The Tower
of Babel

After the great Flood, Noah's three sons and their wives had many more children and grandchildren. Soon there were many people in the world, but once again, people began to do bad things. They started to build a very tall tower so they could make a name for themselves and try to be more important than God. At that time, everyone spoke the same language. God didn't want people to become too proud by thinking they didn't need him, so he "confused their speech" (Genesis 11:7; CCC 57). After that, they spoke different languages. Since they couldn't understand each other, they couldn't finish building the tower. Soon, the people divided into different groups and settled in different cities scattered all over the earth. The tower became known as the Tower of Babel, and the word *babel* means "confused speech."

These stories from the Early World time period show us that God will continue to make a way of salvation so that people can choose to follow him. God wants us to trust and obey him so that he can protect us and give us many wonderful blessings. Abel's sacrifice was pleasing to God because he had a sincere and thankful heart. Noah's ark sheltered and protected the life and goodness that God brought into the world, while the Tower of Babel showed the weakness of people as they tried to make their own way to God. They wanted to build a tower that would stretch up to heaven, but they didn't realize that God has a better way to get to heaven. It is through trusting in God and following his Way, through Jesus Christ, that we will be satisfied.

What do you think?

1. In what ways does God protect you?

2. What does it mean to have a thankful heart?

3. What would the world be like if God hadn't saved the animals?

I will make you a great nation
and I will bless you.
– Genesis 12:2-3

Chapter Four

God Chooses Abraham to Become the Father of Many

Narrative Book: Genesis 12–50

Bible Reading Checklist

- Genesis **12**:1-9; **13**:5-12; **14**:17-20   God promises Abram land, descendants, and worldwide blessing

- Genesis **15**; **17**:1-19   God makes a covenant with Abram

- Genesis **18**; **21**:1-13   The angels visit; the birth of Isaac

- Genesis **22**:1-18   The sacrifice of Isaac

- Genesis **24**   Isaac marries Rebekah

Genesis 12:1-9; 13:5-12; 14:17-20

God Promises Abram
Land, Descendants, and Worldwide Blessing

One of Noah's sons was named Shem. Shem was the great, great, great, great, great, great, great (seven greats!) grandfather of a man named Abram. One day, God told Abram to take his family, their animals, and all their belongings and move from the city of Ur to a new land. Then God made a wonderful three-part promise to Abram (Genesis 12:1-3). God promised (1) to show Abram a new land, (2) to make Abram's name great through many descendants, and (3) that Abram would be a blessing to all the families of the world. This three-part promise provides a framework for the Bible story as it leads to fulfillment in Jesus Christ. Abram obeyed God. He took his wife, Sarai, and his nephew Lot and moved to the land of **Canaan.** Abram and Sarai settled in a hilly area in the land of Canaan about a thousand miles from Ur, and Lot's family settled outside of a town called Sodom. At that time, there were many small kingdoms in the land, and they fought with each other. Lot's family members were taken as prisoners during one of the fights. When Abram heard that Lot's family had been captured, he and some of his men rescued them at night. On the way back home, Abram met a king named Melchizedek. He was the king of Salem, the place we now call **Jerusalem.** Melchizedek was a king of peace and a priest of God Most High. He brought out bread and wine, and he blessed Abram with them. Abram then gave him one-tenth of everything he owned.

Genesis 15; 17:1-19

God Makes a
Covenant with Abram

Circumcision

When Abram was ninety-nine years old, God promised to protect him and to reward him greatly, but Abram wondered how that could be since he had no children. So God took Abram outside and said, *"Look toward heaven, and number the stars, if you are able to number them … So shall your*

22

descendants be" (Genesis 15:5). Then God made a covenant with Abram promising that he would make him the father of many people. When God made this covenant with Abram, God changed his name to *Abraham*, which means "father of many nations." God also changed Sarai's name to *Sarah*, which means "princess." Abraham promised to dedicate all his children and grandchildren and all the following generations to God and to obey all of God's laws. All of the men and boys would be **circumcised** (dedicated to God) as a sign of this covenant (Genesis 17:24).

Genesis 18; 21:1-13

The Angels Visit

After God promised to give Abraham and Sarah a son, he sent three angels to announce it. Sarah laughed when she heard this because she thought she and Abraham were too old to have any children! But the angels assured her that next year at that same time, she and Abraham would have a son. Then Abraham walked with the three angels down toward Sodom, where Lot lived. On the way, God told Abraham that the people in Sodom and Gomorrah had become very evil, constantly sinning against God. Because of this, their cities would soon be destroyed. Abraham

thought about all the people living there, and about his nephew Lot and his family. Abraham begged God to save the city for the sake of the righteous people living there. God promised to save the city if he could find just ten people that obeyed God and lived good lives. Sadly, there were not any righteous living there except for Lot and his family. Lot and his daughters escaped just before the cities were destroyed.

The Birth of Isaac

Just as the angels had predicted, Abraham and Sarah gave birth to their son and named him Isaac, which means "laughter." When Isaac was eight days old, they circumcised him as a covenant sign that he was dedicated to God. Isaac grew into a fine boy.

Genesis 22:1-18
The Sacrifice of Isaac

God wanted to help Abraham strengthen his faith, so God tested him by asking Abraham to bring Isaac up to the mountain of **Moriah** and offer him as a sacrifice. Abraham agreed to do it, and he sadly prepared to give up his beloved son. As father and son climbed the mountain together, Isaac asked his father where the lamb was for the sacrifice. Abraham assured his son that God would provide. Abraham built an altar and laid Isaac upon it, believing that even if he sacrificed

his beloved son on the altar, God could raise him from the dead (Hebrews 11:19). Just as Abraham lifted a knife into the air, an angel of the LORD said, *"Do not lay your hand on the boy!"* (Genesis 22:12). God saw that Abraham was willing to do what he had asked, no matter how difficult. Greatly relieved, Abraham took Isaac off of the altar. Looking around, he saw a ram caught in the bushes. Abraham sacrificed the ram in place of his son. Then God reminded Abraham once again that because he trusted God and obeyed him, God would bless him with many grandchildren and great-grandchildren, and they would live in the land God gave them, and all the nations of the earth would be blessed through them.

Genesis 24

Isaac Marries
Rebekah

When Isaac was grown, Abraham told his servant to go back to Abraham's old city called Haran, about four hundred miles north of Canaan, to find a wife for his son, Isaac. Abraham's servant traveled the long way to Haran and found a beautiful girl there named Rebekah. She and her family agreed to let Abraham's servant take her back to the land of Canaan to marry Isaac. Isaac was happy to marry Rebekah, and he loved her very much. Their marriage shows us that love is a decision. Isaac chose to love her by an act of his own free will. That is why a wedding Mass includes the exchange of vows in which the man and woman promise to love each other until death parts them (CCC 1626–1628).

What do you think?

1. Why does God sometimes make us wait for things?

2. How do you trust God in your own life?

3. How would you feel if you had to move from your home?

I am your brother, Joseph, whom you sold into Egypt.
And now do not be distressed, or angry with yourselves,
... for God sent me before you to preserve life.
– Genesis 45:4-5

Patriarchs

Chapter Five

God Blesses Issac, Jacob, and Joseph

Narrative Book: Genesis 12–50

Bible Reading Checklist

☐	Genesis **25**:19-34; **27**; **28**:1-19	Jacob tricks Esau and dreams of a ladder
☐	Genesis **29**–**30**:24	Jacob marries and has children
☐	Genesis **32**:22-32; **35**:10-29	Jacob wrestles with God
☐	Genesis **37**; **39**–**41**	Joseph in Egypt
☐	Genesis **42**–**46**:4; **49**:1, 8-10	Joseph and his brothers

Jacob
Tricks Esau

Isaac and his wife, Rebekah, had a difficult time having a baby, much like Abraham and Sarah. Finally, they had twin boys they named Esau and Jacob. One night, Rebekah dreamed that her older son, Esau, would serve Jacob, her younger son. This was opposite of the custom at that time, when the birthright of inheritance was always given to the oldest son. As they grew up, Esau became a skillful hunter, while Jacob liked to stay near the tents, tending to the sheep. One day, Esau came home very hungry as Jacob was cooking some stew.

"Let me have some of that or I will die!" said Esau.

"I will trade this food for your birthright," answered Jacob.

This would mean that Jacob would now be considered the oldest and be the one to lead the family after Isaac's death. The son who received the birthright received a double portion of land and possessions for his inheritance. Esau made the trade and eagerly ate the stew.

A few years later, when their father, Isaac, was ready to die, Isaac asked Esau to make him a meal of wild game, promising to give Esau the blessing of the firstborn. Rebekah heard this, and while Esau was out hunting, she helped Jacob trick his father into believing that Jacob was Esau so that Jacob would receive the blessing. Jacob even covered his arms with animal skins to make them feel like Esau's hairy arms. Since Isaac was almost blind, he didn't know that he had blessed Jacob until Esau returned from hunting.

"Please bless me, too!" Esau begged his father, but Isaac told him he could only give one blessing. Esau was furious with Jacob, so Rebekah warned her favorite son to flee to her family's hometown of Haran. Rebekah was sad to see Jacob leave, but she hoped he would find a good wife and be safe. While he was on the way to Haran, he stopped to sleep and had a wonderful dream.

Jacob Dreams of a Ladder

Jacob dreamed of a ladder that reached all the way to heaven, with angels walking up and down on it. God stood at the top of the ladder, and he spoke to Jacob in the dream. God promised Jacob that he would bless him with many children, and that he would always be with Jacob and keep him safe in the land he gave to Abraham and Isaac. When Jacob woke up, he built an altar there and named the place *Bethel*, which means "house of God."

Genesis 29–30:24

Jacob Marries
and Has Children

When Jacob arrived in Haran, he fell in love with a girl named Rachel, the daughter of his Uncle Laban. Jacob asked Laban if he could marry Rachel. Laban said yes, but only if Jacob would agree to work for him for seven years, which he did. When the seven years were over, the wedding finally took place. When Jacob lifted the bridal veil from his new bride's face, though, he saw not Rachel but her older sister, Leah! Laban had tricked Jacob into marrying Leah, because it was the custom for the oldest daughter to marry first. Jacob had to work another seven years in order to marry Rachel. At that time a man could have more than one wife. During the years that Jacob worked for Laban, he had ten sons. When his eleventh son, Joseph, was born, the first child of Rachel, Jacob packed up all his belongings and moved his family back home to Canaan. Laban did not want them to go, but Jacob, Rachel, Leah, and all their children and helpers left in the night.

Genesis 32:22-32; 35:10-29

Jacob Wrestles
with God

One night, on the way back to Canaan, Jacob met a man outside with whom he wrestled until morning. Just as Jacob was winning the wrestling match, the man touched him on the hip and it went out of joint. Thinking that the man was an angel of God, Jacob asked the man to bless him. The man told Jacob that his name would be changed to *Israel*, which means "one who prevails with God." Then God renewed with Israel the covenant promises he had made with Abraham and Isaac. In the land of Canaan, Jacob's twelfth son, Benjamin, was born, but Rachel died during the birth, and they buried her in Bethlehem. The twelve sons of Jacob were named Reuben, Simeon, Levi, Judah, Issachar, Zebulun, Dan, Gad, Asher, Naphtali, Joseph, and Benjamin. Later we will see how the families of each of these twelve sons become large tribes of people called Israelites because they are descendants of Jacob, who is also named Israel.

Genesis 37; 39–41

Joseph in Egypt

The years passed. Jacob loved his twelve sons very much. His favorite was Joseph, the first son of Rachel. He gave Joseph a special ornamented coat with sleeves, but when his brothers saw it, they became envious. Joseph shared two unusual dreams with his family, revealing that one day his brothers would bow down to him as though he was a king. His angry brothers threw him into a pit and then sold him to a band of **Ishmaelite** traders. Then they went home and lied to their father, telling him that wild animals had killed Joseph. Jacob tore his clothes because he was so upset that Joseph was gone. Meanwhile, the Ishmaelite traders took Joseph to **Egypt** and sold him to a man named Potiphar, who worked for the pharaoh, the king of Egypt.

Potiphar liked Joseph and let him work in his home. But Potiphar's wife got angry with Joseph, and had him thrown into jail. While he was in jail, Joseph prayed to God for strength and wisdom. Two other prisoners, a butler and a baker of the pharaoh, had troubling dreams one night. Joseph interpreted their dreams correctly. "Please tell the pharaoh about me," Joseph asked the butler when the butler was released from the jail.

Two years later, the pharaoh had a confusing dream, so he brought Joseph up from prison because the butler remembered Joseph's gift and told the pharaoh about him. Joseph asked God to help him, and then he told the pharaoh what the dream meant. Joseph explained that there would be seven years when all of Egypt would grow more than enough food for everyone, followed by seven years of bad crops, when they would not be able to grow enough grain to feed anyone. Joseph advised the pharaoh to store up the extra grain from the seven good years, so that they would have enough food for the seven bad years. The pharaoh was so impressed with Joseph's wisdom that he made him the second highest ruler in all of Egypt! Only the pharaoh had more authority than Joseph.

Genesis 42–46:4; 49:1, 8-10

Joseph and His Brothers

When the seven bad years came, Joseph's brothers in Canaan ran out of food and went to Egypt to buy some of the extra grain. Joseph was in charge of selling the grain, so they had to bow before Joseph and ask for his permission. While they didn't recognize him, Joseph knew right away that they were his brothers. He asked them to bring the youngest, Benjamin, with them the next time they came for grain. When they came back with Benjamin, Joseph surprised them all by telling them that he was their brother, the one they had sold into slavery. They were amazed to see him! They were very sorry for how they had treated Joseph, and they were glad that he forgave them.

When Joseph's father, Jacob, learned that he was alive in Egypt, Jacob was overjoyed. He moved his family and servants down to Egypt to be close to Joseph, who could make sure they had enough to eat during the famine years. Then Jacob became sick, and he realized that he was near the end of his life. He called his twelve sons to his bedside, and he blessed each of them. He blessed his fourth son, Judah, with a special blessing, saying that someday a great ruler would come from his family line, whom we know later in the Bible to be Jesus. When Jacob died, his sons buried him in the cave of Machpelah in the land of Canaan where Abraham and Isaac were also buried. After that, Jacob's sons, their children, grandchildren, and great-grandchildren stayed in Egypt for about four hundred years.

What do you think?

1. Have you ever had a very strange dream?

2. What blessings has God given your family?

3. How do you live patiently with God's plans for your life?

And Moses said to the people, "Remember this day, in which you came out from Egypt, out of the house of bondage …"
– Exodus 13:3

Chapter Six

God Delivers
the Israelites from
Egyptian Slavery

Narrative Book: Exodus

Bible Reading Checklist

☐	Exodus **1–2** The birth and adoption of Moses
☐	Exodus **3–4** The burning bush
☐	Exodus **5**:1-13; Read one chapter from Exodus **7–10**; Exodus **11–12**:39 The ten plagues and the Passover
☐	Exodus **13**:17–**15**:10 The crossing of the Red Sea
☐	Exodus **16**:1-18; **17**:1-7 God provides manna and water

Exodus 1–2

The Birth and Adoption of Moses

The descendants of Jacob, called **Israelites,** lived for many years in the land of Goshen, the land given to Joseph for his family to dwell in Egypt. A new pharaoh came to power that did not know Joseph or his large family, so he made them all work as slaves. That pharaoh did not want the descendants of Israel to keep growing, so he ordered that any new baby boy should be thrown in the Nile River. However, a mother named Jochebed came up with a plan to save her baby boy. Her husband, Amram, was the great-grandson of Jacob, and the grandson of Levi. Jochebed put her baby in a papyrus basket, like a little ark, and placed it among the reeds on the riverbank. Her daughter, Miriam, the baby's sister, followed the basket and watched as the daughter of Pharaoh found the basket floating in the water. Pharaoh's daughter knew that the baby was one of the Israelites' children, but she wanted to adopt him. Miriam stepped forward and offered to find a woman to take care of the baby until he was older and could be returned to Pharaoh's daughter. Pharaoh's daughter named him *Moses,* which means "I drew him out of the water." Jochebed raised Moses until he was ready to live in Pharaoh's house.

Moses grew up in Pharaoh's household as Egyptian royalty. He knew about the harsh treatment of the Israelite slaves, and he once saw an Egyptian master beating a slave. Moses wanted to save the slave, so he killed the Egyptian and hid the body in the sand. Fearing the anger of Pharaoh, Moses ran away from Egypt and stayed in the land of Midian. There, he married a woman named Zipporah, daughter of a man named Jethro. Moses lived with Jethro and his family for about forty years and helped them tend their flocks of sheep.

Exodus 3–4

The Burning Bush

While Moses was tending the flocks on Mount Horeb, also called **Mount Sinai,** he came upon a bush that was on fire, but it wasn't burning up. God called to Moses from the bush, saying, "*I am the God of your father, the God of Abraham, the God of Isaac, the God of Jacob*" (Exodus 3:6). God told Moses that he had heard the cries of the Israelites in Egypt. He remembered his covenant, and he told Moses that he would lead the Israelites out of Egypt into a land flowing with milk and honey.

God chose Moses to be the one to lead them out of slavery in Egypt. But Moses asked God, "What if the Israelites don't believe that I should be their leader?" God replied, "Tell them that the God of your fathers has sent you, and **I AM WHO I AM.**" Moses felt afraid that no one would believe him. Like shepherds in his day, Moses

carried a long, sturdy wooden rod, or staff. God told Moses to throw his staff on the ground, where it changed into a snake. When Moses touched it, it turned into a staff again. He was to use this miraculous sign when he went to Pharaoh. Moses was also afraid to speak, so God chose his brother Aaron to go with him.

Exodus 5:1-13; Read one chapter from Exodus 7–10; Exodus 11–12:39

The Ten Plagues

Moses and Aaron went to Pharaoh and said, "The God of Israel says to let the people go for a three days' journey into the desert to offer sacrifice to the Lord." Now, Pharaoh's heart was hard, so instead of letting them go, he gave the Israelites even more work. "Now you have to make the same number of bricks, but you have to gather your own straw!" ordered Pharaoh.

Soon, Moses and Aaron returned to Pharaoh to ask again and to show him a sign from God. Aaron threw his staff down, and it changed into a snake. Pharaoh's magicians responded by throwing down their own staffs, and each was also changed into a snake, but Aaron's snake swallowed their snakes. Still Pharaoh remained stubborn, just as God had told Moses.

Since Pharaoh's heart was hard and he would not listen, God sent ten **plagues** upon Egypt. The first plague was water turned to blood. The Egyptian magicians did the same, so Pharaoh would not listen to Moses and Aaron. The second plague was frogs. The Egyptian magicians made frogs appear, too. Pharaoh told Moses that if God took the frogs away, then he would let the people go. When God took the frogs away, Pharaoh changed his mind and would not let the Israelites go. The third plague was gnats; the fourth plague was flies; and the fifth plague was a pestilence, which made all the Egyptians' animals sick. The sixth plague was boils, which caused sores on the Egyptians' skin. The seventh plague was hail that destroyed many crops. The eighth plague was locusts that ate what crops were left. The ninth plague was three days of darkness. Through each of these signs from God, Pharaoh remained stubborn and would not let the Israelites go.

The Passover

God brought one more plague upon the Egyptians, the tenth plague, which caused death to all the firstborn in the land of Egypt. God told the Israelites that they would be saved if they sacrificed a lamb and used its blood to mark their doorposts and lintels. God also instructed the Israelites to ask their Egyptian neighbors for silver and gold, which they did. For their meal that evening they should eat the lamb with unleavened bread and bitter herbs, while being ready to leave Egypt quickly. This was the first Passover. Every firstborn son in Egypt died that night, but the Israelites were saved by the blood of the lamb on their doorposts. God had told them, *"When I see the blood, I will pass over you"* (Exodus 12:13). Pharaoh's son also died, and at last Pharaoh let the Israelites go. They quickly gathered their belongings and journeyed away from Egypt and their slavery.

The Crossing of
the Red Sea

Almost immediately, Pharaoh changed his mind and chased the Israelites with his army toward the Red Sea. By the time he caught up to them, God told Moses to raise his staff, and when he did, the water was split in two. The Israelites were able to walk between the two walls of water on dry land with the Egyptians in fierce pursuit. When the Israelites had safely reached the other side, God told Moses to stretch out his hand over the sea, and the water closed over the Egyptians. The Israelites celebrated God's victory over the Egyptians with singing and dancing. The Israelites were safe on the other side, but now they were in a desert with no food or water.

God Provides
Manna and Water

The Israelites began complaining to Moses about being hungry. God told Moses that he would give them bread from heaven each day. In the morning, the Israelites gathered fine flakes of bread, called **manna,** which tasted like honey. In the evening, God sent them quail. The Israelites complained again and said they were thirsty. Again, Moses asked God what to do. God told Moses to take his staff and strike the rock. As soon as he hit the rock, water flowed out for the people to drink. God had indeed kept his covenant with his people. He freed them from slavery, protected them from death, and gave them manna and water so that they could live while they were in the desert.

What do you think?

1. What would it be like if your family was not allowed to go to Mass?

2. How would you feel crossing on the dry land between two giant walls of water?

3. What food does God provide us with at Mass?

4. What does it mean to listen to God's call?

All that the LORD has spoken we will do, and we will be obedient.
– Exodus 24:7

Chapter Seven

God Forms the Israelite Nation

Narrative Book: Exodus

Bible Reading Checklist

☐	Exodus **19**	The Israelites hear God at Mount Sinai
☐	Exodus **20**	The Ten Commandments
☐	Exodus **24–25**:22; **31**:7-11	Moses on Mount Sinai
☐	Exodus **32**; **34**:1-9, 29-35	The golden calf
☐	Exodus **40**	Moses sets up the Tabernacle

The Israelites
Hear God at Mount Sinai

The Israelites walked in the wilderness until they came to an area called Sinai. They set up their tents and stayed there while Moses went up the mountain. When the people looked up at the mountain, they could see it was covered with smoke, shaking and thundering, which was a sign of God's presence. The people stayed away from the mountain while Moses spoke with God, because they were afraid of the smoke and thunder and in awe of the LORD.

Exodus 20
The Ten Commandments

God gave Moses ten laws called *commandments*, to let the Israelites and us know what we need to do to be freed from the slavery of sin and to live with the blessings of life (Exodus 20:2-17; Deuteronomy 5:6-21; CCC 2052).

The first three commandments show us how to love God.

The next seven commandments show us how to love one another.

1. I AM THE LORD YOUR GOD. YOU SHALL WORSHIP THE LORD YOUR GOD AND HIM ONLY SHALL YOU SERVE.

2. YOU SHALL NOT TAKE THE NAME OF THE LORD YOUR GOD IN VAIN.

3. REMEMBER TO KEEP HOLY THE SABBATH DAY.

4. HONOR YOUR FATHER AND YOUR MOTHER.

5. YOU SHALL NOT KILL.

6. YOU SHALL NOT COMMIT ADULTERY.

7. YOU SHALL NOT STEAL.

8. YOU SHALL NOT BEAR FALSE WITNESS AGAINST YOUR NEIGHBOR.

9. YOU SHALL NOT COVET YOUR NEIGHBOR'S WIFE.

10. YOU SHALL NOT COVET YOUR NEIGHBOR'S GOODS.

God also gave Moses many other laws, which are recorded in the book of Leviticus. Then Moses came down the mountain. At the foot of Mount Sinai, Moses sacrificed young bulls and sprinkled some of the blood on the people as part of the covenant that God was making with the Israelites. God promised to make the Israelites into a mighty nation of priests. The people agreed to obey all that the LORD had commanded them to do.

Exodus 24–25:22; 31:7-11

Moses on
Mount Sinai

Then Moses took his helper, Joshua, back up the mountain to talk to God again. While he was there, God gave him the plans to build a dwelling place for God, or **Tabernacle,** out of the materials they had brought with them from Egypt. Moses stayed on the mountain for forty days. God himself wrote the Ten Commandments onto two stone tablets for Moses to carry down to the people.

Exodus 32; 34:1-9, 29-35

The Golden Calf

Unfortunately, because Moses was gone so long, trouble began brewing at the bottom of Mount Sinai. The Israelites went to Aaron and told him to make a god for them to worship. Aaron agreed to help them make a statue of a false god. He told them to put all their gold jewelry together. They melted it down, and from this he made a golden calf for them to worship! They worshiped the idol instead of the true God. When Moses came down the mountain and saw all the people dancing around the golden calf, he was so angry that he broke the two tablets of the Ten Commandments by throwing them on the ground. Then he threw the golden calf into the hot fire and punished the people for disobeying God. The men from the tribe of Levi helped Moses, so from then on, priests could only be from the tribe of Levi.

Moses loved the people even though they had sinned. He prayed for them and asked God to have mercy on them. God listened to Moses, forgave the people, and promised to go with them across the desert as they traveled. Then the LORD told Moses to make two more tablets of stone for God to write the Ten Commandments again. This restored the covenant between God and his people. When Moses came back down from Mount Sinai, his face was shining and radiant because he had talked with God!

Exodus 40

Moses Sets Up
the Tabernacle

After Moses gave the people the plans for building the Tabernacle, everyone worked carefully to make everything exactly as God wanted it. They made the tent, the tables, and the altars, put up the lamps, and sewed the clothing for the priests. They built the **Ark of the Covenant** to hold the tablets of the Ten Commandments. The Ark was a beautiful, large box covered with gold and decorated with statues

of two angels, also made of gold. God told Moses to anoint Aaron and his sons as priests with oil so they could offer sacrifices in the worship space. When everything was prepared, Moses blessed the Tabernacle by offering sacrifices to God. Moses and Aaron and his sons washed their hands and feet in the large bowl called a *laver* each time they went into the meeting tent or approached the altar. This meant that they were approaching God, who is holy, while remembering their own need of cleansing.

(Catholic churches have holy water fonts at their entrances to remind people of their baptism so that they might approach the sanctuary with a clean heart.)

To show Moses and the Israelites that God's presence was with them in the desert, a cloud covered the meeting tent and the glory of the LORD filled the Tabernacle. The Israelites stayed camped in one location until the cloud rose from the Tabernacle. Then they would pack up all their tents and the Tabernacle, and they would travel on through the wilderness until the cloud stopped. In the daytime, they followed the cloud, and at night, they would see fire in the cloud to light the way. That way, the whole nation of Israel, One Holy Nation, followed God as he led them through the desert. God continued to feed them with manna every day.

What do you think?

1. Why do we need to follow the same commandments today that God gave to Moses?

2. In what places do you feel that you are in the presence of God?

3. What happens when we don't obey God?

4. How does God show his presence in your daily life?

The LORD bless you and keep you.
– Numbers 6:24

Chapter Eight

The Israelites Follow God in the Desert

Narrative Book: Numbers

Bible Reading Checklist

☐	Numbers **1**:1-3, 47-54; **3**:1-4; **6**:22-27 Numbering of the Israelites and Aaron's blessing
☐	Numbers **11**:1-6; **13** The Israelites complain; twelve scouts are sent to Canaan
☐	Numbers **14** Failure to trust God leads to forty years of wandering
☐	Numbers **17** Aaron's budding rod
☐	Numbers **20**:1-13; **27**:12-22 Moses strikes the rock twice; God chooses Joshua
☐	Optional: Numbers **22–24** Balaam and the donkey

Numbering of the Israelites
and Aaron's Blessing

As the Israelites prepared to leave Mount Sinai to go to the **Promised Land** of Canaan, God asked Moses to count the people. Moses gathered the twelve tribes of Israel: Reuben, Simeon, Judah, Issachar, Zebulun, Ephraim, Manasseh, Benjamin, Dan, Asher, Gad, and Naphtali. Remember that these tribes were descendants of Jacob's twelve sons from the time of the Patriarchs. Joseph's descendants were divided to form the tribes of Ephraim and Manasseh, named for Joseph's two sons. The tribe of Levi was not counted in this group because they were priests and would live among the other tribes in certain cities. While the other tribes had armies, the Levites had the duty to take care of the holy vessels of God in the Tabernacle. These vessels were the bowls, cups, lamps, and other items used to worship God.

Then God gave Moses and Aaron a special blessing to say over the Israelites:

"The Lord bless you and keep you!
The Lord make his face to shine upon you, and be gracious to you!
The Lord lift up his countenance upon you, and give you peace!"

– Numbers 6:24-26

As the Israelites traveled, the Lord went ahead of them with a column of cloud by day or a column of fire by night. Manna continued to be present as food for the people to gather. By these signs, the Lord never left the Israelites.

What do you think?

1. When have you gotten a chance to do something over?

2. Tell about a time you were chosen to do an important job.

3. Why do we sometimes grumble about life in spite of God's goodness?

Be strong and of good courage ... for the LORD your God is with you wherever you go.
– Joshua 1:9

Chapter Nine

The Israelites Enter the Promised Land

Narrative Book: Joshua

Bible Reading Checklist

☐	Joshua **1**	Joshua: Israel's new leader
☐	Joshua **2**	Rahab hides the spies
☐	Joshua **3**; **4**	Israel crosses the Jordan
☐	Joshua **6**; **10**:1-15	The fall of Jericho; the sun stands still
☐	Joshua **21**:41-45; **24**:1-28	Covenant renewal

Joshua 1
Joshua:
Israel's New Leader

God told Joshua that he would stay with him wherever he went. He told Joshua to be strong and courageous and to obey all the laws that Moses gave them so that Joshua and all of God's people would be successful in the land of Canaan, the Promised Land. God said they should study the Law every day and do everything that is written in it, and again, he told Joshua to be strong and brave. So Joshua told the people what God said and asked them to get ready to move. He told them what to pack and when they would go. The people told Joshua that they would obey him and God, just as they had obeyed Moses before him.

Joshua 2
Rahab
Hides the Spies

Then Joshua sent two of his men into the land and told them to secretly find out about the city of Jericho. The men went out and spied on the city. They had to be very careful, because the king of Jericho didn't want them to come. He did not want the Israelites to live there. The two spies went to the house of a woman named Rahab, and she was very kind to them. When she heard that the king wanted to arrest the men, she hid them on the roof of her house so they could escape. Rahab trusted God and she knew that the spies were from the people of God. She asked them to save her family from the battle that was about to happen. The two spies gave Rahab their promise that she and all her family would be safe from the coming battle of Jericho. The spies told her to tie a scarlet cord in her window as a signal for the soldiers so they would know who to save. Scarlet is a very bright shade of red, so they would be able to see it easily. Then the two men went back to Joshua and told him that the people in Jericho were afraid of the Israelites and that God would help them win.

Joshua 3; 4

Israel
CRosses the JoRdan

The priests, carrying the Ark of the Covenant, led the whole group down to the Jordan River. When the priests stepped into the water, it stopped flowing and piled up on one side, leaving a dry path, so the people could cross the Jordan on dry land to enter the Promised Land. Twelve men each took a large stone out of the river so Joshua could set them up in a pile as a memorial. In the future, when children would ask their fathers, "What do these stones mean?" then they could tell them, "Israel passed over the Jordan on dry ground." God dried up the waters to let them pass, just as he had caused the Red Sea to part so the Israelites could escape from the Egyptians.

Joshua 6; 10:1-15

The Fall
of JeRicho

The city of Jericho was surrounded by a high and strong wall. God told Joshua how the Israelites should take the city. The priests were to carry the Ark of the Covenant out in front of all the Israelites as they marched around the outside wall of the city once a day for six days. Then on the seventh day, they marched around the city seven times. On the last time around,

the priests blew on trumpets and all the people shouted. Amazingly, the wall around the city fell down so that all the people could go in. The spies saw the scarlet cord that Rahab had hung out of her window, and they saved her and her family from the walls that were crashing down. Rahab and all her family were kept safe because she had helped the spies and all of the Israelites. Rahab eventually married an Israelite named Salmon, of the tribe of Judah, and she became the great-great-grandmother of David and an ancestor of Jesus.

The Sun
Stands Still

Soon after the battle of Jericho, the people from a small city of Gibeon made an alliance with the Israelites, meaning that they would be friends, live in the same land, and protect each other. However, when five neighboring Amorite kingdoms heard about the alliance, they became afraid and decided to band together to attack Gibeon. Joshua's men came back to camp and said that the people of Gibeon were in trouble because the Amorite kingdoms were trying to kill them. Joshua prayed and God told him to be courageous because he was with him and would give the Israelites victory over the Amorites. As Joshua led a surprise attack, God threw great hailstones down from the sky on the enemy armies. Then God caused the sun to stand still until Joshua and his men could rescue all the people in Gibeon. They praised God and thanked him for making the sun and moon stand still so the day would last long enough for everyone to be saved.

Joshua 21:41-45; 24:1-28

Covenant Renewal

Joshua and the Israelites came into the Promised Land to inherit what God had promised them. Twelve tribes each settled into their own territories, which were named after the sons of Jacob: Naphtali, Issachar, Benjamin, Simeon, Asher, Zebulun, Gad, Dan, Reuben, and Judah; and for the two sons of Jacob's son Joseph: Ephraim and Manasseh. One tribe, Levi, did not receive its own territory because they, the Levites, were designated for priestly duties. Instead, they were given forty-eight cities to live in from among each of the twelve territories. There was peace in the land of Israel for many years after the settlement of the territories. When Joshua was an old man, he became tired and sick. He called a meeting with all the leaders and judges of Israel and he told them to keep all the laws of the Book of Moses, to obey God, and to be very brave. He reminded them of all the good things God had done for them and all the promises

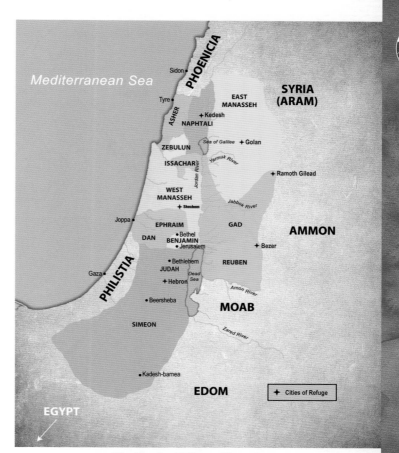

The Twelve Tribes of Israel

God had kept for them. He warned the people not to worship other gods, but to keep the faith in the one true God and to be faithful to him, just as he was faithful to them. The people all promised to obey God, and to make it official, Joshua wrote down their agreement in the Book of the Law of God. Then he set up a memorial stone by the sanctuary where they kept the Ark of the Covenant, as a reminder so people would see it and remember their promise to obey God. Then the people all went back to their own homes, and Joshua died peacefully at the age of 110.

What do you think?

1. What are some of the responsibilities that your priest has?

2. Have you ever made a promise to God? Have you kept it?

3. How can we trust in God to work through us to accomplish his will?

In those days there was no king in Israel; every man did what was right in his own eyes.
– Judges 17:6

Chapter Ten

The Judges Lead the Israelite Tribes

Narrative Book: Judges
Supplemental Book: Ruth

Bible Reading Checklist

☐	Judges **2** Israel is unfaithful to God's covenant
☐	Judges **4–5**:5 Deborah the judge
☐	Judges **6–7**; **8**:28 Gideon the judge
☐	Judges **13**; **16**; **21**:25 Samson the judge
☐	Ruth Ruth becomes part of the lineage of the Messiah

Israel Is Unfaithful
to God's Covenant

The twelve tribes of Israel settled into the parts of the Promised Land allotted to them. God had told them to conquer the Canaanites completely, but instead of driving them out, they lived among them. They shared the land with the Canaanites, and they soon began to follow their ways and worship the false gods the Canaanites worshiped. Some of the Israelites married people from Canaan and forgot about their covenant with the God of Abraham, Isaac, and Jacob. The Tabernacle that had once been in the center of the Israelite camp in the wilderness was set up in a place called Shiloh in the territory of Ephraim. For most of the Israelites, it was a far journey to go there to worship. Seven different times the Israelite tribes struggled with their enemies, and each time God sent leaders called judges to rescue them. The judges were brave leaders in battle who led the Israelite tribes when their enemies attacked them. After God would rescue them, the Israelite tribes would live peacefully for a while. However, the Israelite tribes would once again forget about their covenant with God and return to worshiping the idols of the Canaanites.

Judges 4–5:5

Deborah
the Judge

One of the judges was a woman named Deborah, who would sit beneath a palm tree to give counsel. The Canaanite king Jabin, who ruled from the city of Hazor, captured the nearby Israelites and treated them cruelly for twenty years. Deborah called for a man named Barak to go to the tribes of Naphtali and Zebulun to gather an army.

Barak brought ten thousand men to Mount Tabor and chased out the enemy army, which was led by Sisera, the commander. Sisera ran away and hid in a tent, but a woman recognized him and put him to death. The Israelites defeated the king of Hazor and lived again in peace with Deborah leading them.

Judges 6–7; 8:28

Gideon
the Judge

After forty years of rest, the Israelites were punished for their sins by being placed under the power of the Midianites for seven years. When they cried out in **repentance** to the LORD, God heard their cry and agreed to grant the Israelites salvation through another judge named Gideon.

Gideon was unsure of God's call because he was the youngest member of an unimportant family in the tribe of Manasseh. To test God, he put a fleece (or sheepskin) onto the ground and said, "If in the morning the dew is only on the fleece and the ground is dry, then I know that I should lead the Israelites." The next morning the ground was dry, and the fleece was full of water. Gideon asked for yet another sign, which God gave to him the next morning by making the fleece dry and the ground wet. With these signs, Gideon trusted in the LORD and prepared to answer his call. Next, he looked for men to help him fight against the Midianites. He chose three hundred men who drank from a stream by lapping water from their hands instead of those who leaned over the water to drink. Gideon gave each soldier a clay jar with a torch inside and a horn. When darkness came, the small army surrounded the Midianite camp, and then all at once they smashed their pots, waved their torches, and blew on their horns to make lots of noise. The Midianites became terrified and ran away, because they thought there was a huge army attacking them. Gideon's little army had won the battle! After the Israelite victory over Midian, there was peace for forty years.

Judges 13; 16; 21:25

Samson
the Judge

God sent Samson as the judge to deliver the Israelites from the fighting with the Philistines. Samson was a gift to his parents because they had no children for many years. They raised him with the special vow of a **Nazirite.** Part of the vow was to never cut his hair. Samson, whose name means "sunshine," grew to be one of the strongest men around. He fought many battles against the Philistines. Unfortunately, Samson fell in love with a Philistine woman from Gaza named Delilah. Her name means "nighttime." The leaders of the Philistines told Delilah they would pay her money if she would find out the secret of Samson's strength. They wanted to throw him in prison. Selfishly, Delilah agreed to the plan. Several times she asked Samson to tell her the secret of his strength. Samson then told her that he would become weak if he were tied up with seven fresh bowstrings, so

Chapter Eleven

The Israelites Ask for a King

Narrative Book: 1 Samuel

Bible Reading Checklist

☐	1 Samuel **1–2**:26; **3**	Samuel the prophet
☐	1 Samuel **4**:1-11; **5**:1-5; **7**:1-6; **8**	Capture of the Ark; Israel asks for a king
☐	1 Samuel **9–10**:1	Samuel anoints Saul, the first king of Israel
☐	1 Samuel **15**:10-23; **16**	Samuel anoints David as king of Israel
☐	1 Samuel **17–18**:9; **31**:1-6	David defeats Goliath; death of King Saul

Samuel
the Prophet

A man named Elkanah, and his wife, Hannah, went to the Tabernacle at Shiloh to bring offerings to the LORD. Hannah began to cry from her deep sadness while she prayed, because she didn't have any children. She asked God to give her a son, and she promised that if she had a son, she would give him back to the LORD to live in the Tabernacle and work with the priests. Eli the priest saw her praying and asked her why she was so upset. When Hannah told him, Eli blessed her and said, "Go in peace; God will answer your request." By the next year, Hannah's prayer was answered when she had a baby boy whom she named Samuel. When the boy was old enough, Hannah brought him to the Tabernacle to live there and help the priests. Hannah sang a song of praise and thanksgiving to God, and later on, God blessed Hannah and Elkanah with five more children. Hannah and Elkanah visited the Tabernacle every year and brought Samuel a new linen robe to wear while he helped Eli, the priest.

Samuel was growing up and learning a lot of things from Eli. One night while he was sleeping, Samuel heard someone call, "Samuel! Samuel!" He thought it was Eli's voice. Samuel got up and ran to Eli and said, "Here I am, for you called me." But Eli hadn't called for Samuel, so he sent Samuel back to bed. That happened three times before Eli finally realized that it was God's voice calling for Samuel. Eli told Samuel to answer the voice by saying, "Speak, LORD, for your servant is listening." Samuel obeyed Eli and went back to bed. The LORD God called to Samuel again, and this time Samuel answered, *"Speak, LORD, for your servant is listening"* (1 Samuel 3:9-10). From then on, whenever God would speak to Samuel, Samuel would listen carefully and then tell the people what God had said. He became a faithful **prophet.**

1 Samuel 4:1-11; 5:1-5; 7:1-6; 8

Capture of
the Ark

At one point, when the Israelites were fighting the Philistines again, the elders thought it would be a good idea to bring the Ark of the Covenant into battle to help them win. Instead, they lost the battle and many Israelites were killed. The Philistines captured the Ark and put it into one of their temples, but in the morning, the idol of their god, Dagon, had fallen onto its face as if bowing before the Ark. The Philistines became afraid of the Ark and passed it from city to city until they decided to send it back to Israel on an ox cart. It ended up in the town of Kiriath-Jearim and stayed there for twenty years.

Israel Asks
for a King

When Samuel became an old man, the people began to turn away from God again. They asked Samuel to appoint a king over Israel so they could be like other nations around them who had their own kings. Samuel didn't want to appoint a king over Israel because their king should be God alone. But God told Samuel to give the people what they wanted.

1 Samuel 9–10:1

Samuel Anoints
Saul, the First King of Israel

God told Samuel to find a man named Saul and anoint his head with oil to show that Saul would become the king. Samuel obeyed God and anointed Saul as the first king of Israel. He stayed with Saul for many years and gave Saul advice about how to act as king. There were many wars, and Saul needed to be a good military leader in order to protect the people from the surrounding nations that fought with them. Saul led well in the early years of his reign, but later he became careless and began to disobey God. He stopped listening to Samuel and did things his own way. He decided he would make a sacrifice on an altar instead of waiting for Samuel the priest to do it as God had instructed him. God was displeased because Saul did not obey. Therefore, God told Samuel to anoint another king to take Saul's place.

1 Samuel 15:10-23; 16
Samuel Anoints
David as King of Israel

David was a young shepherd boy who played songs on his harp and cared for sheep in the fields. God told Samuel to go to Bethlehem to the house of a man named Jesse to find the boy David. He should pour oil on his head to show that David would be the next king of Israel to replace Saul. Samuel did as God asked, and God's Holy Spirit filled David that day. After his anointing, David entered into Saul's service as his armor-bearer. David also played his harp for Saul to soothe the king when he was distressed.

David's brothers followed Saul into battle against the Philistines in the Elah Valley. During this time, David continued to tend his father's sheep. One day, David brought food to his older brothers on the battlefield and watched an enormous Philistine named Goliath yell curses at the Israelites and against God. "Let one of you come out and fight me. Whoever wins will be the winner of this battle," shouted Goliath. When David heard the giant's insults, he wanted to challenge him.

1 Samuel 17–18:9; 31:1-6
David
Defeats Goliath

David went to King Saul and told him that he wanted to fight the giant Goliath. He was confident that God was with him so he wasn't afraid. David had killed lions and bears while watching over his father's sheep. Saul gave him permission to fight Goliath, and he even gave David his armor to wear. When David put on the armor, however, it was so big and heavy that he couldn't even walk! David took off the

armor and remained in his regular clothes as he went to a brook to pick out five smooth stones to use in his sling. Then he went to the battleground and saw Goliath there, towering over everyone and yelling threats against the Israelites. When Goliath saw David, he laughed at him and threatened to kill him, but David trusted God. He carefully took a stone out of his pouch, placed it into the sling, and let it fly toward Goliath. That stone hit the giant squarely in the head and he fell over, completely defeated! God had saved the Israelites through the faith of young David.

Death of
King Saul

David became well-known because of that heroic battle, and the people loved him. King Saul's son Jonathan became David's best friend. However, King Saul became very jealous of David. In the years that followed, he watched David's every move. Saul even tried to have him killed. David spent many years running away from Saul's men and hiding in caves. Finally, there was a terrible battle with the Philistines on Mount Gilboa, and Saul's sons were killed while fighting. Saul was also wounded in the battle. When he saw that his sons had been killed, he became so upset that he fell upon his own sword and killed himself. David and all Israel mourned the death of their first king.

What do you think?

1. What would be a good time in your day to be quiet and listen for God's voice?

2. Did you ever ask for a gift thinking it would satisfy you forever? What happened to that gift?

3. What does it mean to obey God's law?

And your house and your kingdom shall be made sure for ever before me; your throne shall be established for ever.
– 2 Samuel 7:16

Chapter Twelve

God Builds a House Through David and Solomon

Narrative Books: 2 Samuel, 1 Kings

Bible Reading Checklist

☐	2 Samuel **1**:1-16; **2**:1-10; **5**:1-12	David becomes king of all Israel
☐	2 Samuel **6**; **7**:16	David brings the Ark to Jerusalem
☐	2 Samuel **11**–**12**:15	David sins and repents
☐	1 Kings **1**:28-40; **3**:1-15	Solomon is anointed king and asks for wisdom
☐	1 Kings **8**:1-21; **9**:1-9; **11**:7-13	Solomon builds a Temple for God

2 Samuel 1:1-16; 2:1-10; 5:1-12

David Becomes
King of All Israel

After King Saul's death, the people of Judah came to David and anointed him king over all of Israel. He was thirty years old when he began his reign as king. King David and his men captured Jerusalem from the Jebusites by crawling through a water tunnel into the city. He made Jerusalem the capital of his kingdom and built a palace there.

2 Samuel 6; 7:16

David Brings
the Ark to Jerusalem

Jerusalem became the capital of the kingdom of Israel. David brought the Ark of the Covenant into the city with joyful singing and dancing, like a holy parade. David danced in the procession so that all the people would rejoice as the presence of God came into their city. David was so filled with emotion that he wanted to build a great temple to house the Ark in which God's presence dwelled. David wanted the Ark to sit in a beautiful building instead of in a tent. A messenger from God informed David that he would be given a son who would build this Temple. Then the worship of God would move from the Tabernacle of Moses at Shiloh to Solomon's Temple in Jerusalem.

 For David's faithfulness, God made a covenant with him. God did not ask David to build a house for him. Instead, God wanted to build a house for David. At the beginning of salvation history, God made a covenant with Abraham, promising to make his name great through countless descendants through whom God would bless all the earth (Genesis 22:15-18). Now God made a covenant with his anointed king, David, to establish a royal kingdom that would be known as the house of David. One of David's descendants would be God's own son, Jesus, the promised Messiah who would bring salvation to all the world.

2 Samuel 11–12:15

David
Sins and Repents

David ruled as a good king for a long time. Once, however, while his armies were away fighting, David fell in love with another man's wife. Her name was Bathsheba. David took her into his palace and arranged to have her husband killed in battle. When David recognized the evil of his sins of murder and adultery, he wholeheartedly repented. He was terribly sorry for what he had done, and he longed for a chance to be close to God again. God knew that David's heart was changed, and God forgave David for his sins. David wrote many psalms in the Bible including one that shows us his repentant heart. *"Create in me a clean heart, O God, and put a new and right spirit within me"* (Psalm 51:10). Then David married Bathsheba and they had a son named Solomon.

1 Kings 1:28-40; 3:1-15

Solomon Is Anointed King
and Asks for Wisdom

David had other sons, but he assured Bathsheba that her son Solomon would be the next king. When David was very old, he had Zadok the priest and Nathan the prophet blow trumpets to announce David's decision about Solomon as his heir. Then they led Solomon on David's donkey to a special place where they anointed him with oil as the king to sit on David's throne. The people were very happy about the announcement, and they rejoiced greatly for their new king.

As King Solomon's royal power was established, God came to him in a dream and asked him what gift he would like to receive. Solomon answered that he wanted the gift of wisdom more than anything else. God was pleased with Solomon's request and gave him wisdom to tell the difference between right and wrong. King Solomon is attributed with writing many wise sayings like those found in the book of Proverbs:

Trust in the LORD with all your heart, and do not rely on your own insight.
In all your ways acknowledge him, and he will make straight your paths.
Be not wise in your own eyes; fear the LORD, and turn away from evil.
It will be healing to your flesh and refreshment to your bones.

– Proverbs 3:5-8

1 Kings 8:1-21; 9:1-9; 11:7-13

Solomon
Builds a Temple for God

King Solomon wanted to build a house for the LORD, a temple that would be suitable for the LORD God. Therefore, when the country was at peace and people felt secure, Solomon started building a beautiful temple in Jerusalem on Mount Moriah where Abraham and Isaac had made a sacrifice long ago. After the Temple was completed, the priests brought the Ark of the Covenant and placed it in the inner sanctuary of the Temple. Two golden angels, or **cherubim,** sat atop the Ark with their wings spread open as a throne for God. Just as the glory of the LORD had filled the Tabernacle in the wilderness, so did the glory of the LORD fill the Temple in Jerusalem, which became the center of worship for all of Israel.

Then God renewed the covenant that he had made with Solomon's father, David. He told Solomon that this kingdom would last forever, but that King Solomon and all the people of Israel would need to obey God and always keep his commandments. God warned them not to worship other gods, because this new house would be destroyed if they turned away from the LORD God. King Solomon was happy with the Temple he had built for the LORD. Then he built more buildings and walls around many cities in Israel. Finally, Solomon had so much money and land that he became known as not only the wisest king, but also the richest. Though Solomon was a good and wise king who built the Temple for the LORD, at the end of his life he did not act so wisely and kept too much wealth for himself. He also let many of his wives worship false idols. Like his father, David, he wasn't perfect, but both he and his father foreshadowed the perfect King God had promised would come to Israel someday. That King, of course, is Jesus.

What do you think?

1. Who do you know that is very wise?

2. Imagine what you might see if you walked into the Temple that Solomon built.

3. How do you show God you are sorry when you have made a wrong choice?

If this people go up to offer sacrifices in the house of the LORD at Jerusalem, then the heart of this people will turn again to ... the king of Judah.
– 1 Kings 12:27

Chapter Thirteen

The Kingdom of Israel Divides

Narrative Books: 1–2 Kings
Supplemental Books: Hosea, Joel, Jonah

Bible Reading Checklist

☐	1 Kings **11**:1-29; **12**; **16**:23-34 The kingdom divides
☐	1 Kings **17** Miracles of Elijah the prophet
☐	1 Kings **18**:17-46 Elijah and the prophets of Ba'al
☐	2 Kings **2**:1-22 Elisha succeeds Elijah
☐	Hosea **11**; Joel **2**:1-14 Rebellion and prophecy of judgment
☐	Optional: Jonah Jonah and the big fish

1 Kings 11:1-29; 12; 16:23-34

The Kingdom Divides

After King Solomon died, his son Rehoboam became king. A bad decision by King Rehoboam caused a division of the Kingdom of Israel into north and south. Rehoboam had asked his advisors to help him decide how to govern the people of the kingdom. The older advisors warned him not to make the people work too hard, but the younger advisors told King Rehoboam to treat the people harshly and make them labor harder than they had for King Solomon. Rehoboam listened to the younger advisors and told the people that he would increase their burdens so they would have to work harder than before. The people became angry, and ten of the twelve tribes of Israel refused to let him be their king.

Instead, they chose a man named Jeroboam to rule them. The ten tribes who followed Jeroboam broke apart from the other two tribes and formed the Northern Kingdom, referred to in the Bible as *Israel*. King Rehoboam was left to govern only two tribes, Judah and Benjamin, which formed the Southern Kingdom, referred to in the Bible as *Judah*. The ten tribes of the Kingdom of Israel were in the northern part of the Promised Land, and the Kingdom of Judah was in the south. Jerusalem and the Temple were located in the Southern Kingdom of Judah. The Northern Kingdom set up false places of worship in the cities of Dan and Bethel because they no longer traveled to Jerusalem to worship in Solomon's Temple. This division caused the two kingdoms to be at war with each other for many years.

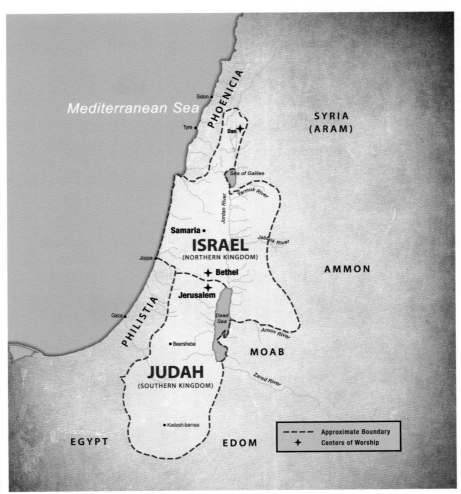

Map of the Divided Kingdom

1 Kings 17

Miracles of
Elijah the Prophet

Many years after Jeroboam's rule in the Northern Kingdom of Israel, Ahab, son of Omri, came to the throne. King Ahab married a woman named Jezebel who worshiped the false gods of **Ba'al** and **Asherah.** Jezebel commanded that God's prophets be hunted down and killed.

At this time, there was a prophet of God named Elijah, who wore a hairy garment with a leather belt as a sign of his calling as a prophet (2 Kings1:8). Prophets sometimes tell what can happen in the future. The prophet Elijah went to King Ahab and told him that there would not be any rain for three years in the land because of the altars to Ba'al and Asherah. God told Elijah to stay by a brook where ravens would bring him bread and meat during the famine. When the brook dried up because of the drought, Elijah went to a widow's house to find food and drink. She only had enough oil and flour for one more meal for herself and her son. She made Elijah a cake of bread, and miraculously God made the jar of flour and pitcher of oil last for three years, until the end of the drought! Later, when the widow's son became sick and died, Elijah took him by the hand and raised him from the dead by the power of God.

1 Kings 18:17-46
Elijah and the
Prophets of Ba'al

Elijah continued to prophesy to King Ahab and told him that there had been no rain because Ahab had left God and worshiped the false gods Ba'al and Asherah.

"Let's have a contest to see who is the true God," Elijah said to the king. "Bring your 450 prophets of Ba'al and 400 prophets of Asherah to Mount Carmel and we will each offer a sacrifice to his god. The sacrifice that burns without us lighting a fire will be the god that we will serve."

So they all went to Mount Carmel to set up two altars. Ahab and Jezebel's prophets called on Ba'al to send fire. All day long, their prophets danced, prayed, and even cut themselves with knives in order to try to get the attention of their false god, but there was so answer. Next, Elijah prepared his altar for the sacrifice. But first he poured water over it and all around it, so that it was drenched. When Elijah called upon the LORD, God immediately sent fire down from heaven that burned up the whole sacrifice. When the people of Israel saw this, they all knelt down and shouted that the LORD is God! Then it began to rain and the long drought was over. Queen Jezebel was angry when she heard that Elijah had defeated all her false prophets, so Elijah, fearing for his life, ran to the Southern Kingdom of Judah for safety.

2 Kings 2:1-22
Elisha
Succeeds Elijah

Later, God spoke to Elijah to find a man named Elisha, who would be Elijah's servant and would later take his place as prophet. Elisha became Elijah's faithful helper and learned how to be a prophet by working with him for several years. Finally, the time came for Elijah to go and be with God forever. The two prophets walked by the Jordan River. Elijah took off his cape, rolled it up, and hit the water with it. The river divided so that the two prophets could cross over it on dry land. Then they looked up, and suddenly a chariot of fire swooped down and picked up Elijah. He sailed into heaven on the chariot of fire, and Elisha was left alone on the ground. He picked up the cape that Elijah had dropped, and he went back to Samaria, the capital of the Northern Kingdom, to work as a prophet of God. Elisha helped many people as God worked miracles through him. After Elisha died, the ten tribes of Israel continued to suffer under the rule of evil kings even though Elisha had told them to repent.

Rebellion and
Prophecy of Judgment

Other prophets of God, like Hosea and Joel, warned the kings of the Northern Kingdom of Israel that they must follow the ways of God or the army of the **Assyrians** would defeat them. The prophets told them that God earnestly wanted them to turn their hearts back to him so he could save them from their enemies. God loved his people very much, but they rejected him.

Optional: Jonah

Jonah and the Big Fish

Jonah was another prophet, but unlike Elisha, he was not always obedient to God. There was a city called Nineveh, where the people worshiped false gods and treated each other very badly. God told Jonah to go to Nineveh and tell them to repent. Jonah didn't want to go. Instead, he got in a boat headed in the opposite direction! When a severe storm hit, Jonah realized he was running away from God, so he told the sailors to throw him overboard. After they cast him over the side, Jonah sank in the water until a giant fish swallowed him whole. He spent three days and nights in the belly of the fish. While he was in the belly of the fish, Jonah repented and promised to obey God. The fish threw him up onto shore, and Jonah headed straight to Nineveh to proclaim God's Word to the people there. When they heard Jonah's proclamation, the people became very sorry for what they had done. They promised to stop doing evil things. Then God forgave them in his great mercy.

What do you think?

1. How does God want us to act toward our family and friends?

2. When people disagree, what is a good way to settle it?

3. Who can give you good advice when you are trying to make a difficult decision?

But you shall fear the LORD your God, and he will deliver you out of the hand of all your enemies.
– 2 Kings 17:39

Optional: Jeremiah 18:1-17; 31:1-14, 31-34

The Prophet Jeremiah
Warns Israel and Judah

Jeremiah was a great prophet during this time who prophesied to both the Kingdoms of Israel and Judah. God spoke through him to tell people that they were being ungrateful to God and that they were suffering because they had forgotten to obey his laws. Jeremiah used the image of God as a potter, who would mold his people like clay into the good and wonderful people he created them to be. Jeremiah prophesied about a coming day when God would make a new covenant with Israel and Judah and that their love for God would come from the heart.

What do you think?

1. What are the things in life that might lead us away from God?

2. What happens to a group when their leader chooses to do good things?

3. How do you stay mindful of the Ten Commandments in your life?

By the waters of Babylon,
there we sat down and wept,
when we remembered Zion.
– Psalm 137:1

Chapter Fifteen

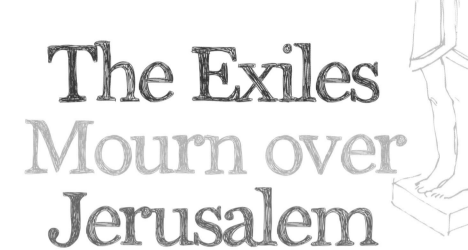

The Exiles Mourn over Jerusalem

Narrative Book: 2 Kings
Supplemental Books: Jeremiah, Psalms, Daniel

Bible Reading Checklist

☐	2 Kings **17** Assyria conquers the Northern Kingdom; foreign possession of Samaria
☐	2 Kings **25**:1-21; Jeremiah **38**:1-6; Psalm **137**:1-4 Babylon conquers the Southern Kingdom
☐	Daniel **2** Daniel interprets the king's vision
☐	Daniel **3** Three men in the fiery furnace
☐	Daniel **6** Daniel and the lion's den

Assyria Conquers the Northern Kingdom

In the year 722 BC, the king of Assyria conquered the Northern Kingdom of Israel. Three years earlier the Assyrians invaded the area and robbed and looted their homes, stealing the things they used for idol worship. The capital of the Northern Kingdom, Samaria, was built on a hill, so it was hard to capture, but the Assyrians surrounded Samaria and would not let them get food or water. The Israelites were starving and dying so they eventually gave up their city. The Assyrians killed King Hoshea and carried the people away as slaves. The ten tribes of the Northern Kingdom of Israel were lost among the foreign nations, and they never returned to the Promised Land again.

Foreign Possession of Samaria

Then the king of Assyria brought his own people from five foreign lands to settle around the city of Samaria, where the Israelites used to live. They settled into their homes and began living there, worshiping their false gods. When lions came into their towns and attacked them, they sent word to the king of Assyria that God had sent the lions to kill them because they did not know how to worship the God of Israel. Therefore, the king of Assyria sent some of the exiled priests back to Samaria so that they could teach the people their religious customs. The people did not really learn how to worship the God of Israel. Instead, they only copied what the priests did and continued to worship their own false gods at the same time. They did not follow the commandments God gave to his people through Moses, especially the first commandment that says, *"You shall have no other gods before me"* (Exodus 20:3). This group of people came to be known as the **Samaritans.**

2 Kings 25:1-21; Jeremiah 38:1-6; Psalm 137:1-4

Babylon Conquers
the Southern Kingdom

Since the Southern Kingdom had been constantly fighting with the tribes in the Northern Kingdom and had turned away from God so many times, they, too, had become weak. The prophet Jeremiah warned the people that they would be conquered because of their refusal to turn away from their false gods. The people became angry at this prophecy and threw Jeremiah into a muddy *cistern,* or well. Finally, King Nebuchadnezzar of **Babylon** attacked, captured, and took the people into captivity just as it had happened to the Northern Kingdom many years earlier. The people were carried away

with their hands and feet tied. The king's sons were killed, and King Zedekiah was blinded and thrown into prison in Babylon.

After that, King Nebuchadnezzar's men went to the Temple in Jerusalem and broke into pieces the bronze pillars that King Solomon had made for the house of the LORD. They took the bronze back to Babylon along with all the pots, shovels, and snuffers, the dishes for incense, and all the other sacred vessels used in the Temple. Then they burned down the houses, including the house of the LORD, so that they were completely destroyed. Lastly, they captured the priests that served in the Temple and carried them back to Babylon, where they killed them.

This sad part of the story is called the Exile, because God's people were taken away from the Promised Land and made to live in a foreign place. Only a small group of people remained behind to take care of the vineyards and olive trees. The exiles in Babylon wept for **Zion,** the hill in Jerusalem on which the Temple was built. Their sin had not only led to their separation from their land, but to a separation from God. The name *Zion* came to represent the entire city of Jerusalem as the spiritual center of the people of Israel.

Daniel Interprets
the King's Vision

The people from the Kingdom of Judah became known as the Jewish people. While they were in exile in Babylon, many of the Jewish people still loved God and wanted to worship him properly. One of these faithful people was a young man named Daniel. Daniel was bright and strong, and God had prepared him to be a prophet. King Nebuchadnezzar of Babylon saw how bright he was and took Daniel to work in his royal palace. One night, Nebuchadnezzar had a strange dream. His advisors didn't know how to interpret it, so Daniel offered to pray to God to find out what the dream meant. The dream was about a huge statue. The head was made of gold, its chest and arms were silver, and its stomach and thighs were bronze. The statue's legs were iron, and its feet were made of part iron and part clay. Then someone, not a person, cut out a stone and broke the statue's feet with it so the whole statue broke apart. Daniel explained to the king what his dream meant. He said that the statue represented five kingdoms. The gold head was the Babylonian kingdom, where they were then living. After Babylon, **Persia** would rule, represented by the silver chest and arms. Then Greece, another kingdom, would rise, represented by the bronze belly and thighs, and then Rome, symbolized by the legs of iron. The fifth kingdom, represented by the stone, was the one that God himself would set up. That kingdom would bring an end to all the other kingdoms and last forever. We understand now that the last kingdom is the kingdom of God (CCC 2816–2820).

Daniel 3
Three Men
in the Fiery Furnace

King Nebuchadnezzar was impressed by Daniel's interpretation of his dream and made Daniel ruler over the province of Babylon. But the king was still attached to false gods, and he made a large image of gold, to which he commanded all of the people to bow down and worship. Three Jews in exile, named Shadrach, Meshach, and Abednego, refused to bow down before the idol of the king. When they were brought before Nebuchadnezzar, the king ordered that they be thrown into a fiery furnace for their disobedience. While the three men were in the fire, an angel of the LORD came to be with them and protected them from harm. All of the men blessed God and sang his praises while the flames burned around them. King Nebuchadnezzar was amazed at this miracle, and he proclaimed that the God of Shadrach, Meshach, and Abednego had delivered them. He decreed that from that day forth, no one should ever again say anything against their God.

Daniel
and the Lion's Den

After Nebuchadnezzar, King Darius ruled in Babylon. Daniel continued to be given great responsibility in the court, which made many other people jealous. These officers plotted against Daniel to have the king sign a law that no one could worship anyone but the king. When they found Daniel worshiping God instead, they brought him to King Darius complaining that he had broken the new law and must be thrown into a den of lions. Although King Darius liked Daniel, he could not break his own law and ordered that

Daniel be cast into the den with the lions. God sent his angel to be with Daniel and saved him from death by closing the mouths of the lions. The king was astonished at God's saving power and decreed that everyone in Babylon should honor the living, eternal God.

The Jewish people were in exile in Babylon for seventy years. During their captivity, they had time to remember all of the wonderful things God had done in the past. They had a change of heart and began to understand that God's judgment is always right and his mercy is endless. They looked forward to the day when they would be able to return home to Jerusalem.

> *Look on my affliction and deliver me, for I do not forget thy law.*
> *Plead my cause and redeem me; give me life according to thy promise!*
> *Salvation is far from the wicked, for they do not seek thy statutes.*
> *Great is thy mercy, O Lord; give me life according to thy justice.*
> – Psalm 119:153-156

What do you think?

1. Describe how good things can sometimes come from a bad experience.

2. How do you find courage to do the right thing?

3. Do you ever feel far away from God? How do you become closer to him?

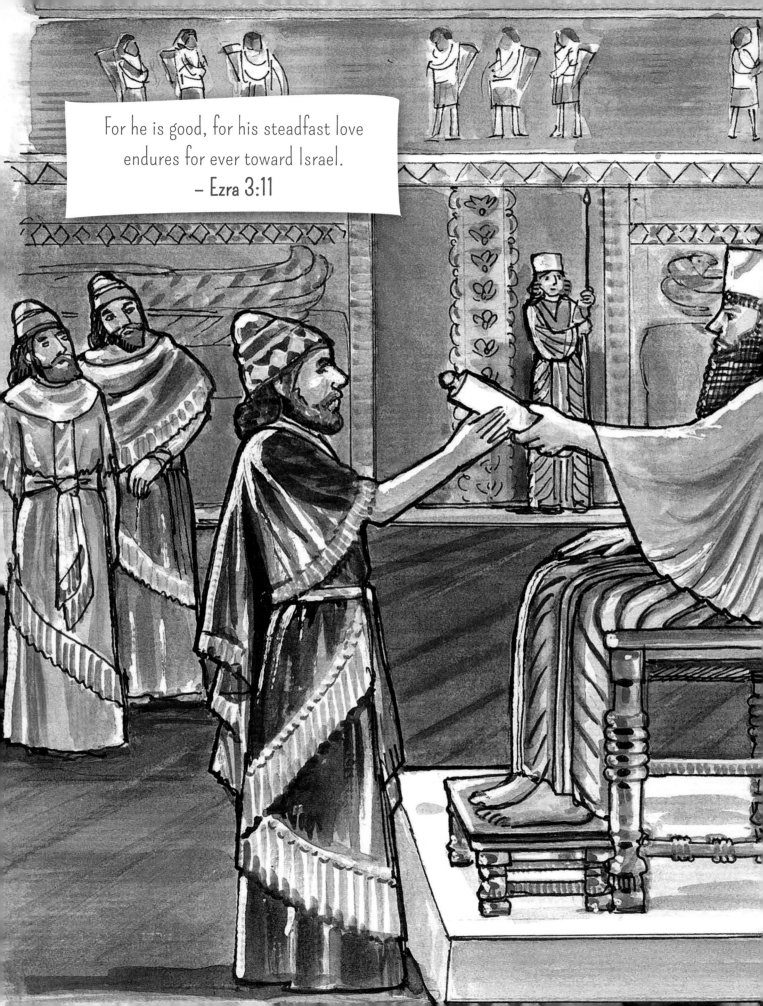

For he is good, for his steadfast love endures for ever toward Israel.
– Ezra 3:11

Chapter Sixteen

The Exiles Return to Jerusalem

Narrative Books: Ezra, Nehemiah
Supplemental Books: Jeremiah, Esther

Bible Reading Checklist

- [ ] Ezra **1**–**2**:2   King Cyrus allows exiles to return

- [ ] Ezra **3**–**4**:4   The foundations of the Temple are laid

- [ ] Ezra **7**:1-10; Nehemiah **1**–**2**:11   Ezra and Nehemiah return to Jerusalem

- [ ] Nehemiah **2**:12-20; **4**   The wall around Jerusalem is rebuilt

- [ ] Nehemiah **8**   Ezra reads the Book of the Law of Moses

- [ ] Optional: Esther   Esther saves her people

Ezra 1–2:2

King Cyrus Allows
Exiles to Return

The Kingdom of Babylon lost its influence, and Persia, led by King Cyrus, became the most powerful kingdom. There were still many exiles from the Kingdom of Judah living as slaves in the land that was once called Babylon and now called Persia. King Cyrus told the exiles to go back to Jerusalem to rebuild their Temple. The house for God that Solomon had built had been destroyed when the Babylonians had invaded, so Cyrus told the exiles to rebuild that Temple and bring offerings to give to God when it was finished. One of the exiles, Zerubbabel, was appointed as governor of the area of Judah. He and Jeshua, the priest, led the exiles back. It was a very exciting time! They brought back the sacred cups and washbasins, gold and silver, and animals for sacrificing to the LORD. The exiles returned to the towns where their families had lived before their capture. After they came back, they gathered in Jerusalem and built an altar so they could start making offerings to the LORD right away. They celebrated the **Feast of Booths** and joyfully worshiped the God of their ancestors.

Ezra 3–4:4

The Foundations
of the Temple Are Laid

Next, Zerubbabel and Jeshua hired masons and carpenters, and bought building materials to repair the Temple. They bought cedar trees from **Lebanon** to use for lumber. They appointed priests from the tribe of the Levites to oversee the work. When the builders finally laid the foundation stone in place, they had a big celebration. The priests came dressed in their holy vestments playing trumpets, while the other Levites followed behind playing loud cymbals, all to praise the LORD with their music. People came from all around to celebrate. Some were very happy and shouted with tears of joy, and others were sad because they remembered their once beautiful Temple. Their shouts of joy and sadness mingled together and were heard by people all around. When some of their neighbors heard the shouting and saw that the returned exiles were beginning to rebuild their Temple, they were jealous. They complained to the new king of Persia, Artaxerxes, and he ordered them to stop. They had to wait until a new king came into power, King Darius, who would let them continue.

Ezra 7:1-10; Nehemiah 1–2:11

Ezra and Nehemiah
Return to Jerusalem

The Jewish people in Jerusalem sent a letter to King Darius after he took the throne and reminded him that many years earlier King Cyrus had given them permission to rebuild the Temple. When King Darius realized this, he made a decree, which is a new law. The decree gave the **Jews** permission to start working again, and it also gave them building materials and supplies for making pleasing sacrifices to God. That was pretty amazing for a foreign king to do. Ezra the scribe led a group of exiles to Jerusalem to continue the work. Once again, they celebrated as they dedicated their work to God with joy. In the months and years following, they remembered to celebrate all of the important holidays like the **Feast of Passover** and the **Feast of Unleavened Bread.** Unfortunately, they forgot one very important law that God had given them in the Ten Commandments. They forgot that they were not supposed to worship false gods. They married people from the surrounding nations and began to worship the gods of those other nations. This was a serious problem, and many people were hurt because of the bad example set by the leaders and priests.

Ezra was a priest from the line of Aaron who helped the people to remember the Law of Moses. While Ezra was praying, people came out and began to cry because they realized what they had done. They were very sorry and decided to make things right again. They turned away from the false gods of the other nations, and sent the wives and children back to their own families in those nations. Then they took an oath, promising to be faithful to God once again. Many more exiles returned to Jerusalem with a prophet named Nehemiah.

Nehemiah 2:12-20; 4

The Wall Around Jerusalem
Is Rebuilt

Nehemiah had heard that the wall of Jerusalem was broken down and the gates
had been destroyed, so he was eager to return and rebuild it. The wall was very
important because it went around the city of Jerusalem to keep the people
safe inside. Many enemies tried to get the people to stop building the wall, but
Nehemiah was brave, and he trusted in the Lord to help them. Finally, the wall
was finished and the city was protected. Parts of this wall are still visible in the city
of Jerusalem today.

108

Ezra Reads the Book
of the Law of Moses

Return

When the wall of Jerusalem had been rebuilt, the people gathered inside the city near the Water Gate to hear something very important. Ezra the priest brought out the Book of the Law of Moses that the LORD had given to the Israelites. Ezra began to read it out loud to everyone who was there: men, women, and children who were old enough to understand the words. Everyone listened carefully and happily as Ezra read out loud. He was reading God's Word to them. When he finished, the priests helped him explain what the reading meant and the people understood. They rejoiced when Nehemiah and Ezra told them this was a holy day and that the joy of the LORD would be their strength. Following the reading, everyone celebrated with shouts of thanksgiving, singing and playing musical instruments! Now that the time of the long exile was over, people were once again free to worship in Jerusalem at the newly rebuilt Temple, and they could read and study the words of the Law of Moses whenever they wanted to. All of these things helped them have a better relationship with God and with each other.

Throughout the time of the Return, God restored the Jews by bringing them back to Jerusalem to rebuild the Temple and the wall around the city. Their joy was renewed while they heard the life-giving words from the Book of the Law of Moses. God had promised many times through his prophets that he would restore his people. God is always ready to bless people and lead them back into the safety of his kingdom.

Optional: Esther

Esther Saves Her People

While many of the Jewish people returned to the land of Israel, some were still in Persia, including a faithful young woman named Esther. Esther, her cousin Mordecai, and their family lived in the city of Susa, capital of Persia. The king of Persia at that time was a wealthy ruler named Ahasuerus, also known as Artaxerxes, who reigned over a vast kingdom. He was kind to the Jewish people living in Persia, but his servant Haman was not. Haman plotted to kill the Jewish people, but God had placed Esther in a position where her bravery and faithfulness saved her people from destruction. Esther had been chosen by King Ahasuerus to be the queen of Persia. When she learned about Haman's plot, she bravely told King Ahasuerus about it. The King loved Esther and her cousin Mordecai, so he put a stop to the evil plans Haman had made. Then he appointed Mordecai as his servant, and all the Jews from that day forth remembered the time with a holiday called **Purim.** Esther's bravery saved the Jewish people from death.

What do you think?

1. What can happen if we only keep the laws of God that we find easy and don't keep the ones that seem hard?

2. Why do we hear the Bible read aloud at every Mass?

3. Is there a place where you experience God's presence with joy?

We will not obey the king's words by turning aside from our religion to the right hand or to the left.
– 1 Maccabees 2:22

Chapter Seventeen

The Maccabees Defend the Faith

Narrative Book: 1 Maccabees
Supplemental Book: 2 Maccabees

Bible Reading Checklist

	Reference	Description
☐	1 Maccabees **1**:1-19	The Greek Empire comes to power
☐	1 Maccabees **1**:20-63	Greek persecution of the Jews
☐	Optional: 2 Maccabees **7**	The woman and her martyred sons
☐	1 Maccabees **2–3**:2	Mattathias and his sons revolt
☐	1 Maccabees **4**:36-59	Purification of the Temple
☐	2 Maccabees **12**:39-45	Prayers for the dead

1 Maccabees 1:1-19
The Greek Empire
Comes to Power

After Persia, Greece became the strongest power in the world. The Greek Empire grew under the military leadership of Alexander the Great, who conquered Persia and then most of the known world. He died in his early thirties, and his empire was divided among his three generals. Greek was the main language spoken during this time in history. Even the Old Testament was translated into Greek around the third century BC. *Hellenism* is a word that describes Greek world culture. The whole world was "hellenized" by Greek customs, language, and religion, which often conflicted with the laws God had given to his people, such as the worship of many **mythological,** or false, gods such as Zeus and Hercules.

1 Maccabees 1:20-63
Greek Persecution
of the Jews

The Seleucids were the Greek people that became the governors of the Promised Land area. A Seleucid ruler named Antiochus Epiphanes ruled over the southern region, now called **Judea,** and Jerusalem. He entered the Jewish Temple and took the sacred vessels away. Antiochus was very cruel and persecuted the Jews. He made a decree to force all the inhabitants of Judea to worship the way the Greeks did by bowing down to idols and offering sacrifices that were forbidden by God for Jews. He sent people to Judea to offer unholy sacrifices on God's altar. Antiochus also would not allow them to circumcise their boys, which was the Jewish sign of their covenant with God. The books of God's Law were burned and people who would not obey the new decree were put to death.

Optional: 2 Maccabees 7

The Woman and Her Martyred Sons

During this time of Greek oppression, many Jews continued to follow the Law of God, rather than obey the laws of the Greeks. One of these heroic Jewish people was a brave mother with seven sons whom she had raised to be faithful to the God of Israel. Antiochus told the mother and her sons that they had to bow to a Greek statue and eat pork, a food forbidden under Jewish Law, or they would be killed. The mother and her sons chose to obey God, and they refused to bow down to the Greek statue or

eat pork. One by one, the sons were killed in front of their mother, but she offered them encouragement, and they remained brave and willing to die for their faith. Finally, after all seven sons were cruelly killed, Antiochus also had the mother killed. They all believed that they would see God after they died (CCC 633–637), so they chose to die rather than disobey God. People who die for their faith are called **martyrs.**

Mattathias and His Sons Revolt

In the town of Modein in Judea, there was a devout priest named Mattathias who had five sons. Some officials sent by Antiochus came to Modein offering silver and gold to people who would make sacrifices of unclean animals to pagan gods. This was forbidden by Jewish Law. Mattathias would not do it, and he would not allow anyone else to do it either. He said, *"Let every one who is zealous for the law and supports the covenant come out with me!"* (1 Maccabees 2:27). This was the start of the Maccabean Revolt. Mattathias killed the government official and chased the others away. Then he and his sons hid in the wilderness because they would be arrested if caught. Many Jews joined them to fight against the Seleucids. After

many years of battle, Mattathias died and his son Judas became the leader. Judas Maccabeus led many fierce battles until the Jewish people won back the city of Jerusalem and once again controlled the Temple.

1 Maccabees 4:36-59

Purification
of the Temple

The Temple was overgrown with bushes and many parts were ruined. The altar had been profaned by the Greeks, so Judas Maccabeus saw to it that it was cleaned and ritually purified by the priests. They rebuilt the stone altar and made new holy vessels and brought back the lampstand and the table that belonged in the Temple. Everyone was so happy that for eight days they celebrated around the Temple with singing and dancing in the streets. Judas declared that this should be celebrated every year. Today this Jewish holiday is called **Hanukkah.**

Prayers
for the Dead

After Antiochus Epiphanes died, his son, named Antiochus Eupator, came to power. Although Eupator said that the Jews should be allowed to live as they pleased, some of the local governors continued to treat the Jews badly. Judas Maccabeus and his soldiers called upon God for help and marched against those who killed the Jews. At the end of one attack, Judas and his men worked together to bury their fellow soldiers who had fallen. They discovered that those who had died were wearing tokens of idols and false gods under their clothing. This is forbidden by the first commandment, which states that we must love our God and must not worship any other gods. Judas was sad that these soldiers had not trusted the LORD God, but he prayed that the sin of those who had died would be forgiven (CCC 1030–1032).

The Maccabean revolt, which lasted about seven years, shows us how people who were devoted to following God were able to fight against the culture that threatened them. The Jews knew what God wanted them to do because they prayed, obeyed God's commandments, and read the Book of the Law. God gave them courage to stand up for their faith.

In our lives today, we must be sure that we do not follow the culture when it leads us away from God. We can also know how God wants us to live by praying, obeying, and studying the Bible and *Catechism*. The same God who gave the Jews courage to stand up for what is right also gives us the courage to do what is right.

This is the last narrative book of the Old Testament. Sadly, the Maccabean dynasty, or **Maccabees,** also known as the **Hasmoneans,** did not last and was conquered by Rome. Judea was ruled by King Herod the Great, while Caesar Augustus was the Roman emperor. Herod fought against the Hasmoneans and took over their outposts. King Herod built many fortresses and also beautified the Temple in Jerusalem not long before Jesus would be born. The stage was set for the King of Kings to come into the world!

What do you think?

1. Why do we pray for those who have died?

2. What are some things in the sanctuary of a church that remind us that it is a holy place?

3. How does God help you do the right thing when others around you are making poor choices?

And behold you will conceive in your womb and bear a son, and you shall call his name Jesus.
– Luke 1:31

Chapter Eighteen

Jesus, Son of God, Is Born of Mary

Messianic Fulfillment

Narrative Book: Luke
Other Gospels: Matthew, John

Bible Reading Checklist

☐	Luke **1–2**	Birth of John the Baptist; the early life of Jesus
☐	Luke **3–4**:30	Baptism of Jesus; temptation of Jesus
☐	Luke **5**; John **2**:1-11	Jesus calls his disciples; Jesus' first miracle
☐	Matthew **5**:1-12; **8**:5-13	Jesus teaches the Beatitudes; Jesus heals the centurion's servant
☐	Luke **9**:1-36	Jesus gives his authority to the Twelve; Jesus feeds the five thousand; the Transfiguration

Luke 1–2

Birth of John the Baptist

A priest named Zechariah and his wife, Elizabeth, were both very old and had no children. While Zechariah was in the Temple in Jerusalem, an angel of the Lord told him he would have a son. This baby would grow up to be John the Baptist, who would tell people to, *"Prepare the way of the Lord"* (Isaiah 40:3). Because Zechariah did not believe the words of the angel, he became unable to speak until the baby was born. Elizabeth named the baby John, and once again Zechariah was able to talk. John grew up to live in the wilderness of Judea. At that time, several groups who wanted to live a life close to God lived together in communities in the wilderness, much like monks live in **monasteries** today. Some of those groups wrote texts that are part of the **Dead Sea Scrolls.**

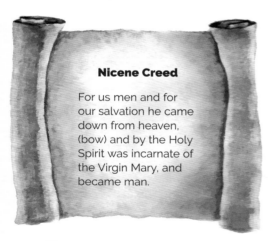

Nicene Creed

For us men and for our salvation he came down from heaven, (bow) and by the Holy Spirit was incarnate of the Virgin Mary, and became man.

First Joyful Mystery
The Annunciation (Luke 1:28)

Second Joyful Mystery
The Visitation (Luke 1:41-42)

The Early Life of Jesus

Before the birth of John the Baptist, the angel Gabriel appeared to a relative of Elizabeth, a young girl named Mary. The angel said, *"Hail, O favored one, the Lord is with you"* (Luke 1:28). Gabriel told Mary that she would have a baby who would be the Son of God and that she should name him *Jesus,* which means "God saves." Mary wondered how this could happen, but she trusted God and said "yes." Then Mary went to visit Elizabeth to share the wonderful news. As Mary arrived, the baby in Elizabeth's womb, John, jumped with joy! Mary stayed with Elizabeth for three months and then returned to Nazareth, where she and Joseph lived.

The Roman emperor, Caesar Augustus, took a **census** of all the people in the Roman Empire. Mary and her husband, Joseph, traveled to Bethlehem to be counted because that was the city of Joseph's family. So, there in Bethlehem, Jesus was born. Mary and Joseph wrapped him in **swaddling clothes** and laid him in a **manger.** The child would also be known as *Emmanuel,* which means "God with us" (Isaiah 7:14; Matthew 1:23). By taking human form, Jesus is God **incarnate** (CCC 464).

Angels appeared to nearby shepherds out in the field saying, *"Glory to God in the highest, and on earth peace to people of good will"* (Luke 2:14; Mass Response). The angels told them that a Savior was born that very night. The shepherds hurried to visit Mary and Joseph and to greet the newborn King.

Days later, Mary and Joseph brought Jesus to Jerusalem to be circumcised, as was the practice for all Jewish boys on the eighth day following their birth. They also presented him in the Temple to fulfill Jewish Law. In the Temple, two prophets recognized that he was the Messiah. An old man named Simeon had been waiting a long time, expecting that Jesus would come to be presented in the Temple. When Mary and Joseph approached Simeon, he took Jesus in his arms and predicted that he would be great. He also cautioned Mary that his greatness would cause her much sorrow. Then a prophetess named Anna came forward and proclaimed that deliverance had finally come to God's people.

The last story we hear of Jesus as a young boy is during the Feast of Passover when he was twelve years old. Jesus and his family traveled to Jerusalem as they did each year for the Feast. After they had participated in the Passover celebration, they headed home to Nazareth, but Mary and Joseph discovered that Jesus was not among the travelers. Worried, they hurried back to Jerusalem and searched many places for him. At last they found Jesus in the Temple, asking questions and giving such wise answers that the elders with whom he

Third Joyful Mystery
The Birth of Christ
(Luke 2:7)

Fourth Joyful Mystery
The Presentation
of Jesus
(Luke 2:22-23)

Fifth Joyful Mystery
The Finding of
the Child Jesus in
the Temple
(Luke 2:48)

spoke were amazed. Mary and Joseph asked Jesus why he had done this, and Jesus replied that he needed to be in his Father's house. However, he obeyed his parents and returned to Nazareth with them. There, Jesus grew from a boy into a man, learning the trade of carpentry from his earthly father, Joseph. He also continued to study the Law of Moses, growing in wisdom until he was ready to start his ministry at about the age of thirty.

Luke 3–4:30

Baptism
of Jesus

When Elizabeth and Zechariah's son, John, grew up, he dressed in a camel hair garment like the prophet Elijah (Matthew 3:4) and preached about the repentance of sins. People came from all around to be baptized by him in the Jordan River, including Jesus. John baptized Jesus, even though John said that he was not worthy to untie Jesus' sandals. When Jesus received **baptism** from John, he allowed himself to be numbered among sinners (CCC 536–537). A dove descended on Jesus as a voice from heaven said, *"Thou art my beloved son"* (Luke 3:22).

First Luminous Mystery
The Baptism of Jesus
(Luke 3:22)

Temptation
of Jesus

Right after his baptism, Jesus went into the wilderness. He spent forty days praying there, and he didn't eat anything, so he became very hungry. The devil came and tried to tempt him with food, power, and riches. Each time, Jesus responded by repeating words from the Bible. Jesus did not give in to the temptations, so the devil left him alone, and angels came to take care of him.

Luke 5; John 2:1-11

Jesus Calls
His Disciples

Jesus came to the town of Capernaum on the shores of the Sea of Galilee where he chose twelve men to follow him. Some of these men were fishermen. He told them not to be afraid, because one day they would be catching people instead of fish! The names of the twelve men he chose were Simon, whom Jesus named **Peter**, Peter's brother **Andrew, James** and **John** the sons of Zebedee, **Philip, Bartholomew, Matthew** the tax collector, **Thomas, James** son of Alphaeus, **Simon**

Sacrament of Holy Orders

125

the Cananaean, **Thaddaeus,** and **Judas Iscariot,** who became a traitor (Luke 6:14-16). All of these men, even Judas Iscariot, were important to Jesus. He chose these men to spread the Good News to everyone.

Jesus' First Miracle

Second Luminous Mystery
The Wedding at Cana
(John 2:1-11)

Not far from Capernaum was the small village of Cana. Jesus and his family were invited to a wedding there. Weddings in those days lasted several days. Toward the end of the celebration, the host ran out of wine, so he had nothing left to give all his guests. Mary, the mother of Jesus, urged Jesus to do something to help. Jesus told the servants to fill some large jars with water and then bring a sample of it to the head steward. They obeyed, and when the steward tasted the water, it had turned into the finest wine.

Matthew 5:1-12; 8:5-13

Jesus Teaches the Beatitudes

Third Luminous Mystery
The Proclamation of the Kingdom
(Matthew 5:1-12)

Jesus went to a nearby hill to preach to his disciples and to all the people who came to hear him. He told them about the kingdom of God and how to be truly happy. He said that people are happy, or blessed, when they are meek, mourning, and hungering for justice. He said people are blessed when they are merciful, pure of heart, and make peace with each other. He also said that people who suffer **persecution** and cruelty because of Jesus are really blessed. Because of all of these things, their reward will be happiness in heaven. Jesus told them to love their enemies and be good to all people, even those who hate them. Jesus taught that it is good to treat others the way we ourselves want to be treated. He encouraged the people to depend on God and not to worry about what to eat or wear. He assured them that everyone who comes to him, hears his words, and obeys them is like a person who builds their house on a firm foundation. The storms of life will not be able to shake them. These teachings of Jesus are the new law of love (CCC 1965–1971).

Jesus Heals
the Centurion's Servant

Jesus spent a lot of time in the town of Capernaum. In that town was a synagogue where he would preach. There was a Roman soldier who was a **centurion,** in charge of a hundred soldiers who were camped near the town. The centurion had donated money to build the **synagogue.** He had a servant that he loved very much, but who had become quite sick. The centurion had heard of the miracles and teaching of Jesus, so he believed that Jesus would heal his servant if he asked. Jesus gladly said he would go to heal the man's servant, but the centurion said, *"Lord, I am not worthy to have you come under my roof; but only say the word, and my servant will be healed"* (Matthew 8:8; Mass Response). Jesus was impressed with the faith of the centurion, and at that moment, the servant was healed.

Luke 9:1-36
Jesus Gives His Authority
to the Twelve

After Jesus had performed many miracles in the region of Capernaum, Jesus then gave his twelve **disciples** his authority to go out and heal the sick and free those troubled by demons. He sent them out with power to heal and to proclaim the kingdom of God.

**Sacrament
of the Anointing
of the Sick**

Jesus Feeds
the Five Thousand

Crowds from miles around gathered near the Sea of Galilee outside Capernaum to hear Jesus teach. After a while, they became hungry. The disciples told Jesus he should send them away to get food, but Jesus told them they should feed the crowd. That seemed impossible to the disciples. They only had five loaves of bread and two fish. Jesus instructed the disciples to have the people sit down in groups. Then Jesus took the five loaves and two fish, looked up toward heaven, and blessed and broke them. He gave them to the disciples to share. About five thousand men plus women and children were able to eat until they were full; then the leftovers were gathered until they filled twelve baskets! This amazing miracle helps us understand how the **Eucharist** feeds the whole Church.

The Transfiguration

Soon after the feeding of the five thousand, Jesus took Peter, James, and John and climbed a mountain in order to pray. While they were on the mountain, the face of Jesus began to glow with a bright light. Moses and Elijah, the prophets from the Old Testament, appeared and stood next to him. The disciples were afraid when a cloud overshadowed them, but the voice of God came from the cloud. He said, *"This is my Son, my Chosen; listen to him!"* (Luke 9:35). Once again, God confirmed that Jesus is the Son of God.

Fourth Luminous Mystery
The Transfiguration
(Luke 9:28-36)

What do you think?

1. What was the result of Mary saying "yes" to God's plan for her?

2. How do you know that Jesus is divine?

3. How do you create personal time to listen to God?

He went on his way
through towns and villages,
teaching, and journeying
toward Jerusalem.
– Luke 13:22

of his actions, he went home to his father. When his father saw him coming, he yelled for joy! He ran out to greet his son, who expressed how sorry he was for the way he had lived. The father welcomed his son and threw a large party to celebrate his return. The older brother was jealous about the party given for his brother, who had behaved so irresponsibly. His father assured his older son that he loved him and told him that he was rejoicing because his lost son had been found! God is like the happy father who welcomes us when we come to him.

Jesus Heals
Ten Lepers

As Jesus journeyed toward Jerusalem for the Feast of Passover, he met a group of **lepers** who were not allowed to be with other people because of their disease. They cried out to Jesus for mercy and Jesus healed them (CCC 2616). Then he told them to show themselves to a priest, as was the custom, to be declared "clean" from the disease. Ten men were healed, but only one turned back to thank Jesus for his kindness. The one who returned to him was a Samaritan and not a Jew. Jesus asked him, "Where are the other nine?" Jesus was surprised that his own people did not thank him for being healed.

Jesus
and the Children

Many of the people who went to hear Jesus teach brought their babies and children with them, hoping that Jesus would bless them. The disciples scolded the people, but Jesus welcomed them all. Jesus said that the kingdom of God belongs to children and to anyone who has a child-like trust and acceptance of God's love.

Luke 18:31-34; 19:1-10

Jesus
Predicts His Passion

At times, Jesus spoke privately with his twelve disciples. As they traveled toward Jerusalem for the Feast of Passover, he told them that when they arrived, everything would happen just like the prophets had foretold (Isaiah 53), that the **Son of Man** (Daniel 7:14) would be beaten and killed but would rise from the dead on the third day. Jesus' bodily suffering, death on a cross, and his resurrection, also known as Jesus' **passion,** was not what the disciples were expecting, so they did not understand what Jesus was trying to tell them. They thought that the Messiah would free the Jews from the Roman government and lead them like King David had done many years ago. They hoped Jesus would become an earthly king.

Matthew 20:29-34

Jesus Meets Zacchaeus
and Heals Blind Men in Jericho

As Jesus and his disciples continued toward Jerusalem, they passed through the town of Jericho and a crowd gathered. A tax collector named Zacchaeus wanted to see Jesus, but because he was short, he wasn't able to catch a glimpse of him over the heads of the people. Zacchaeus ran ahead of the crowd and climbed a sycamore tree. He didn't expect Jesus to look up as he passed and call to him, "Zacchaeus, come down! I'll stay at your house tonight." Zacchaeus was overjoyed, but the other people in the crowd grumbled that Jesus would spend time with

such a sinner. Zacchaeus had become wealthy by cheating people as he collected their taxes. Zacchaeus, however, became a changed man because of Jesus' love. He repented of his sins, returned money he had taken dishonestly, and gave more of his wealth to the poor. Jesus called Zacchaeus a "true son of Abraham," which meant that Zacchaeus now had a heart to follow God and was living the way God wants all his children to live: with a generous, repentant heart and caring for others. Through his repentance, Zacchaeus received the promise of salvation that was made to Abraham, father of the Jewish people, thousands of years before.

As Jesus left the town of Jericho, a crowd continued to follow him. They passed by two blind men, sitting along the roadside, who called out to Jesus asking to be healed. Though the crowd told them to be quiet, they cried out even louder saying, **"Lord have mercy** on us, Son of David!" (CCC 2616; Matthew 20:31; Mass Response). Jesus asked the men what they wanted, and they replied that they wanted their eyes to be opened. Feeling pity for the men, he touched their eyes and they could see again!

Upon reaching Jerusalem, Jesus was ready for the last days of his life on earth. He had chosen twelve men to carry on his mission after he was no longer with them. Jesus also had shown by example and by teachings how his followers could bring healing, truth, and love to the world.

What do you think?

1. Do you have a favorite parable that Jesus told? What is it, and why do you like it?

2. Can you say the Our Father? What does Jesus teach us about forgiveness in this prayer?

3. Describe what it might be like to sit in the lap of Jesus and listen to him tell stories.

And he took bread, and when he had given thanks he broke it and gave it to them, saying, "This is my body which is given for you. Do this in remembrance of me."
– Luke 22:19

Chapter Twenty

Jesus Establishes the New Covenant

Narrative Book: Luke
Other Gospels: Matthew, John

Bible Reading Checklist

☐	Luke **19**:28-48 — Jesus' triumphal entry into Jerusalem
☐	Luke **22**:1-62 — The Last Supper; the Garden of Gethsemane
☐	Luke **22**:63–**24**:12; John **19**:25-27 — Jesus' passion, death, and resurrection
☐	Luke **24**:13-49 / John **20**:19-29 — The risen Lord on the road to Emmaus; Jesus breathes on the disciples; doubting Thomas
☐	Luke **24**:50-53; Matthew **28**:18-20 — The Ascension

Luke 19:28-48

Jesus' Triumphal
Entry into Jerusalem

The last place Jesus spent time teaching was in the city of Jerusalem. When he arrived, Jesus rode a humble donkey into the city, and the people put their coats on the road to carpet the path. They were excited for Jesus to come and shouted, ***"Blessed is he who comes in the name of the Lord! Hosanna in the highest!"*** (Matthew 21:9; Luke 19:38; Mass Response). We repeat these words at Mass during the Eucharistic prayer. We also recite, ***"Holy, holy, holy is the Lord of hosts; the whole earth is full of his glory"*** (Isaiah 6:3; Mass Response).

Although the people of Jerusalem were excited about Jesus' arrival, Jesus wept as he looked over the city and talked about a time to come when the city and the Temple would be destroyed. When he got off the donkey near the Temple, he saw people selling things at unjust prices and failing to treat the Temple as the holy house of God. This made Jesus angry. He drove them out so that the Temple could once again be a house of prayer. Not everyone in Jerusalem wanted to listen to Jesus' teachings. Instead, they wanted to trick him so he would say something that the Roman government would not like and they could have him arrested.

Luke 22:1-62

The Last Supper

Sacrament of the Holy Eucharist

While Jesus was in Jerusalem, the Feast of Passover arrived. Jesus and his twelve apostles were together to celebrate this special meal that recalls the deliverance of the Jewish people from slavery in Egypt. On the night of the first Passover, as told in the book of Exodus, the Israelites were saved from the angel of death by the blood of the lamb, which was painted on their doorposts and lintels. During Jesus' celebration of the Passover meal, he told his disciples how his blood would be shed for a new kind of deliverance. He took a cup of wine, and when he had given thanks he said, *"Take this, and divide it among yourselves; for I tell you that from now on I shall not*

142

drink of the fruit of the vine until the kingdom of God comes" (Luke 22:17-18). Then Jesus took the bread, and when he had given thanks, he broke it and gave it to his disciples saying, *"This is my body which is given for you. Do this in remembrance of me"* (Luke 22:19). Jesus told his disciples that the cup is a new covenant in his blood, which would be shed for everyone. Secretly, before the meal, Judas had made plans to betray Jesus to the Jewish leaders, and he left the meal before it was finished.

Fifth Luminous Mystery
The Institution of the Eucharist
(Luke 22:19-20)

The Garden of
Gethsemane

After they had eaten, Jesus and his disciples went to the Garden of Gethsemane on the Mount of Olives to pray. Jesus was very troubled knowing that soon he would suffer in great agony for the sins of the whole world, so he prayed to his Father in heaven for strength to bear the suffering. Although he knew that what was to come would be very painful, he accepted the will of God. While they were in the garden, a crowd arrived, led by Judas Iscariot. When Judas gave Jesus a kiss, the chief priests and Temple guards arrested Jesus, even though he was innocent, just like the lamb that was sacrificed for the Passover meal.

First Sorrowful Mystery
The Agony in the Garden
(Luke 22:44-45)

Second Sorrowful Mystery
The Scourging at the Pillar
(John 19:1)

Third Sorrowful Mystery
The Crowning with Thorns
(Matthew 27:28-29)

Luke 22:63–24:12; John 19:25-27

Jesus' Passion

Jesus was given a false trial by the Jewish leaders, beaten, and turned over to the Roman authorities. At the command of Pontius Pilates, the Roman guards whipped him. A crown of thorns was then placed on Jesus' head (Matthew 27:29-30), and he was sentenced to be crucified. Throughout the trial and persecution, Jesus never condemned those who hurt him. Finally, Jesus was given a cross of wood to carry to a rocky hill outside the city of Jerusalem. There, Jesus was nailed to the Cross and left to die, along with two criminals. A large crowd of women stayed with Jesus and wept for him in great sadness. One of the crucified criminals joined the soldiers who mocked Jesus, but the second criminal recognized that Jesus was the Son of God. He asked Jesus to accept him as part of the kingdom of God. Jesus assured him that he would join him in heaven that day.

Nicene Creed

For our sake he was crucified under Pontius Pilate, he suffered death and was buried,

Jesus' Death

Along with the apostle John, there were some women standing under the Cross near Jesus, including Mary Magdalene, Mary the wife of Clopas, and Mary, the mother of Jesus. It was very hard for Jesus' mother to see him suffer, but she trusted God. When Jesus looked and saw his mother there, he said to her, "Woman, behold, your son," then to John, "Behold, your mother." He did this in order to give his mother to all of us who believe in Jesus as John did. So John took care of Mary from that moment on.

At about three o'clock in the afternoon, Jesus cried out in a loud voice, *"Father, into thy hands I commit my spirit"* (Luke 23:46). At that moment the earth shook (Matthew 27:51) and the **veil of the Temple** ripped in two. Then

Fourth Sorrowful Mystery
Jesus Carries the Cross
(John 19:17)

Jesus died. We remember the day that Jesus died as Good Friday, but this day wouldn't be "good" at all without the events that happened next. Jesus was buried in a tomb with a large rock covering the entry, but his story wasn't over.

Fifth Sorrowful Mystery
The Crucifixion
(Luke 23:46)

Jesus' RESURRECTION

Nicene Creed

and rose again on the third day in accordance with the Scriptures.

On a Sunday, the third day after Jesus was buried, three women went to the tomb and found that the large stone had been rolled away. An angel appeared to them and told them that Jesus was not with the dead, but that he had been raised. They looked into the tomb and found that his body was not there!

First Glorious Mystery
The Resurrection of Christ
(Luke 24:1-7)

They ran quickly to tell the apostles the amazing news! This is the long-awaited Good News that God promised to Eve in Genesis 3:15, that her offspring would conquer sin and death. The Resurrection is the "crowning truth of our Faith" (CCC 638). It also gives us hope that we, too, will be raised to eternal life (CCC 658).

Luke 24:13-49

The Risen Lord on the Road to Emmaus

On that same Easter day, Jesus appeared to two disciples walking on the road to a town called Emmaus. They did not recognize him as they walked along, telling him all that had happened to Jesus. They had even heard that the tomb was empty, but they did not know how that could happen. Jesus then told them how the stories of Moses and the prophets pointed to the Messiah and why the Messiah had to suffer. As the three travelers approached a village, the disciples invited the stranger to come in to eat with them. Jesus joined them for supper and took the bread, blessed it, broke it, and gave it to them. At that moment the disciples recognized him. Jesus vanished and they could not see him anymore, but they were so filled with joy that they ran all the way back to Jerusalem to share with the disciples what had happened.

We can feel that same joy today when we share in the Eucharistic meal. Jesus is with us each time we receive him in the bread and wine that has been changed into his Body and Blood at Mass.

Jesus Breathes
on the Disciples

Sacrament of Reconciliation

Also on Easter, Jesus came to the disciples in the Upper Room. Thomas was not with them. They were frightened at first, but Jesus said, ***"Peace be with you"*** (John 20:19, 21; Mass Response). Then he breathed on them, giving them the Holy Spirit. He also told them that whose sins they would forgive would also be forgiven by God, and whose sins they did not forgive would not be forgiven by God. This authority that Jesus gave to the apostles has been passed on to priests so that they might administer the sacrament of reconciliation.

John 20:19-29
Doubting
Thomas

When Thomas heard from the other disciples that Jesus had appeared to them, he did not believe it. He said he would only believe if he could actually touch the wounds in Jesus' hands and in his side. Suddenly, Jesus again appeared to the apostles in the Upper Room where they were gathered. Jesus showed Thomas his hands and side, and Thomas believed. Then Jesus told them that people who believe without seeing are blessed. We have not seen Jesus with our own eyes, yet we are blessed because we believe through our faith.

Luke 24:50-53; Matthew 28:18-20
The Ascension

Second Glorious Mystery
The Ascension
(Luke 24:51)

For forty days Jesus appeared to his disciples and continued to teach them. He instructed them to stay in Jerusalem, promising them that the Holy Spirit would come to fill them with power. Then Jesus brought his disciples outside Jerusalem; he raised his hands and blessed them and began to rise into the air. He rose higher and higher, as if he were on a cloud, until no one could see him anymore. He had gone to heaven to be with his Father.

Although the disciples didn't want Jesus to leave, they were full of joy when he ascended because they understood that Jesus would live through them as they shared his love with others.

Jesus' last words to his disciples were to go into the world and make more disciples, to pass on the faith by baptizing people in the name of the Father and of the Son and of the Holy Spirit, and to teach others what Jesus had taught them. Jesus promised them and us today that he would be present until the end of the age.

Nicene Creed

He ascended into heaven and is seated at the right hand of the Father.

Sacrament of Baptism

The Great Commission

And Jesus came and said to them, "All authority in heaven and on earth has been given to me. Go therefore and make disciples of all nations, baptizing them in the name of the Father and of the Son and of the Holy Spirit, teaching them to observe all that I have commanded you; and lo, I am with you always, to the close of the age."

– Matthew 28:18-20

What do you think?

1. Do you get angry sometimes? How can you be angry and not sin?

2. How can you share in Jesus' suffering on the Cross?

3. How would you recognize Jesus if he walked alongside you today?

When the day of Pentecost had come,
they were all together in one place.
– Acts 2:1

Chapter Twenty-One

The Holy Spirit Ignites the Church

Narrative Book: Acts

Bible Reading Checklist

☐	**Acts 1** — The replacement of Judas
☐	**Acts 2** — The day of Pentecost
☐	**Acts 3**:1-16; **4**:1-22, 32-37 — Peter and John heal a lame man; the Church shares
☐	**Acts 5**:12-42 — The disciples witness to the Jewish leaders
☐	**Acts 6**–**8**:4 — The martyrdom of Stephen

Acts 1

The Replacement
of Judas

Since Judas Iscariot had left them, the remaining eleven apostles chose a man named Matthias to take his position. Matthias had followed Jesus as a disciple throughout his ministry.

Acts 2

The Day of
Pentecost

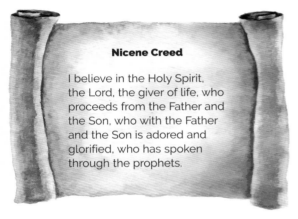

Nicene Creed

I believe in the Holy Spirit, the Lord, the giver of life, who proceeds from the Father and the Son, who with the Father and the Son is adored and glorified, who has spoken through the prophets.

Third Glorious Mystery
The Descent of the Holy Spirit
(Acts 2:4)

Sacrament of Confirmation

The apostles were gathered together in one place for the **Feast of Pentecost,** which was celebrated fifty days after Passover. They were expecting something because Jesus had told them to wait in Jerusalem for the promise of the Holy Spirit. Suddenly, they heard a rushing sound like the wind, and tongues of fire appeared over their heads. Then they began to speak in languages that they hadn't learned before. They were so excited they rushed out into the streets! They spoke to the Jewish pilgrims who were visiting Jerusalem from other nations of the world. Each person heard the wonderful gospel message in his own language. This dramatic experience was a fulfillment of prophecy spoken by the prophet Joel, *"I will pour out my spirit on all flesh"* (Joel 2:28). Thousands of people believed in Jesus through the preaching of the gospel. They were baptized outside the Temple in the purification pools near the main steps. Modern **archaeologists** have uncovered these pools and steps, which can still be seen today. The day of Pentecost is considered the birthday of the **Church** (CCC 2623).

Acts 3:1-16; 4:1-22, 32-37

Peter and John
Heal a Lame Man

On the way to the Temple, Peter and John met a lame man begging for gold and silver. Peter told him that he had something better to offer—healing through Jesus Christ. They performed a miracle as Jesus had done by taking his hand and telling the lame man, in the name of Jesus Christ, to walk. The man was healed and began praising God and leaping about. A big crowd came to see what happened, and they were all astounded! Five thousand people became believers in Christ because of what they had seen. However, some of the priests and **Sadducees** were angry when Peter and John began to preach of Jesus' resurrection because they didn't believe it had happened. They had Peter and John arrested. They were brought before Annas the high priest and Caiaphas. Peter and John were warned not to speak about Jesus again, but they were so filled with the Holy Spirit, they were not afraid to speak the truth that God raised up Jesus whom the religious leaders had crucified with the help of the Romans.

The Church Shares

Nicene Creed

I confess one Baptism for the forgiveness of sins.

Peter and the other believers shared everything with each other. They cheerfully gave all they had to God to support the work of spreading the Good News of Jesus Christ by selling their property and sharing the money with the others. Many people came to hear the disciples preach and to witness God's healing power. When the disciples prayed and laid their hands on people, God would heal them. The Church began to grow in numbers as thousands of people believed and were baptized and filled with the Holy Spirit.

Acts 5:12-42

The Disciples Witness to the Jewish Leaders

Because so many people were now following the gospel of Christ, the high priest and the religious leaders continued to be angry and jealous of the work of the disciples. They arrested them and put them in jail, but the disciples escaped with the help of the Holy Spirit. They went to the Temple and began preaching to the people. The religious leaders asked them why they were still talking about the resurrection of Jesus when they had told them to stop. Peter said that they would obey God rather than any human leader. The religious leaders left them alone for a while after that because one leader, **Gamaliel,** told them that this might be the work of God so they should not stop it.

Acts 6–8:4

The Martyrdom of Stephen

There were so many people becoming believers in Jesus Christ and the Good News about the kingdom of God that the disciples needed to appoint more men to help them. They chose seven men with good reputations, who were wise and full

of the Holy Spirit. The apostles laid their hands on them and prayed over them, naming them **deacons.** One of them was Stephen, who was full of grace and power and spoke with great wisdom.

Once again the religious leaders objected to the preaching of the gospel, so they had Stephen arrested, accusing him of breaking the Law of Moses. Stephen, though, was brave and trusted God to help him speak the truth. Stephen told the high priest and the crowd God's plan of salvation through Jesus Christ, but it only made them angrier, and they began to throw stones at him. As they continued to stone him, Stephen looked toward heaven and told them he could see Jesus standing at the right hand of God. They shouted and crowded around Stephen, dragging him out of the city. A religious leader named Saul was watching and was supportive of the stoning of Stephen. As he died, Stephen prayed that God would forgive his attackers for killing him. Stephen became the first Christian martyr, because he was killed for believing in Jesus. Then Saul began to persecute others who believed in Jesus. He went from house to house, arresting both men and women and throwing them in jail for their faith.

What do you think?

1. What does it mean that the Holy Spirit dwells in you because of your baptism?

2. What are some ways that you share with others?

3. How can you act like Jesus so others can see him in you?

Now those who were scattered went about preaching the word.
– Acts 8:4

Chapter Twenty-Two

The Apostles Spread the Gospel

Narrative Book: Acts

Bible Reading Checklist

☐	Acts **8**:4-40 The apostles spread the gospel
☐	Acts **9**:1-25 The conversion of Saul
☐	Acts **10**; **11**:19-26 Peter's vision of the unclean animals
☐	Acts **12**:1-19; **13**:13-43 Peter's arrest and deliverance; Paul's first missionary journey
☐	Acts **15**:1-21 Council at Jerusalem

Acts 8:4-40

The Apostles
Spread the Gospel

In obedience to Jesus' Great Commission to spread the gospel, the apostles spread out from Jerusalem. Philip went to the city of Samaria and told the people about Jesus the Messiah. Through Philip, God healed many who were sick or possessed by **unclean spirits.** People were eager to be baptized as soon as they heard that Jesus was the Messiah and that God wanted them to turn away from sin and be healed. Peter and John came and laid hands on them so that they could also receive the Holy Spirit. This is the same way that we receive the sacrament of confirmation today. After that, Philip traveled a road that goes from Jerusalem to Gaza, where he met a **eunuch** who worked for the queen of **Ethiopia.** The eunuch had been in Jerusalem to worship and was on his way back home to Ethiopia when he met Philip. Philip told him how Jesus fulfilled the things written in the Old Testament Scriptures about the Messiah. The eunuch listened excitedly and asked Philip to baptize him right away in some water on the side of the road!

Acts 9:1-25

The Conversion
of Saul

The young man Saul, who had encouraged the people to kill Stephen, was still arresting people who believed in Jesus Christ. As Saul was traveling on the road to a town called Damascus to arrest more believers, he was suddenly surrounded by a shining bright light from heaven. Saul fell to the ground and heard a voice call his name and ask him why he was persecuting him. The voice was that of Jesus. When Saul understood that he was attacking Jesus himself and hurting his Church, he repented of his attack on the Church and decided to follow Jesus. As Saul got up he realized he was blind. His friends helped him find his way into town, where he stayed for three days until God sent a disciple named Ananias to him. At first, Ananias did not want to see him because of all the terrible things Saul had done to

the Christians, but reluctantly he went and laid hands on Saul. Instantly, Saul was healed of his blindness and was filled with the Holy Spirit. Saul was so amazed that he got up right away and wanted to be baptized. After Saul's conversion, his name was changed to Paul. He became a powerful teacher who convinced many people that Jesus was the Messiah.

Paul went to stay with a group of disciples that had gone to the city of Antioch. They gathered together regularly to worship God and preach about the gospel of Jesus the Messiah. The disciples in Antioch were the first people in the Church to be called **Christians.**

Peter's Vision
of the Unclean Animals

In the town of Caesarea, there lived a centurion named Cornelius. Although he wasn't Jewish, he loved God, lived a prayerful life, and supported those in need. People who are not Jewish are called **Gentiles.** One day as he prayed, Cornelius had a vision in which an angel came to tell him that God had heard his prayers and he should send some men to the town of Joppa to ask Peter to come to his house. So Cornelius sent three men to invite Peter to come. Meanwhile, in the town of Joppa, Peter had a dream in which a large sheet was lowered from heaven in front of him. There were all kinds of animals on the sheet, including those that Jews were not supposed to eat according to the Law of Moses. In the dream, God told Peter to get up and eat any kind of meat that he wanted. After the dream was over, Peter wondered what it meant. Just then, the men that Cornelius sent came asking for Peter. Peter went with the men to Cornelius' house, and there he saw that Cornelius had faith in God, even though he was a Gentile. Then Peter understood what his dream meant: God wanted the Good News about Jesus to be shared not only with Jews but with the Gentiles, who did not practice circumcision and all of the dietary rules of the Law of Moses. Peter told Cornelius and his household all about Jesus. They believed and wanted to be baptized. Peter baptized all of them, and they were filled with the Holy Spirit. Peter went back to the Church at Jerusalem and told everyone what had happened. They praised God that God's plan of eternal life also included the Gentiles.

Acts 12:1-19; 13:13-43

Peter's Arrest
and Deliverance

At this time, Herod Agrippa, the king, persecuted many Christians. He had Peter arrested and put in prison. Peter was bound in two chains, sleeping in his prison cell when God sent an angel to him in a flash of bright light. Suddenly, the chains fell off his wrists and the angel helped Peter escape. He went straight to the house of Mary, the mother of John (also known as Mark), where several Christians had gathered to pray for him. Peter told them how God had answered their prayers. Then he went to another place so King Herod's men could not find him. The apostles continued to proclaim the Good News about Jesus, and more and more people became believers.

Paul's First
Missionary Journey

Paul traveled to many parts of the world to build God's Church and spread the Good News of salvation. His first journey began in the city of Antioch and continued on to the island of Cyprus. From there, Paul went to Pisidia to another town also called Antioch. There, he spoke to the Jewish people in the synagogue about the history of salvation, telling them how God first revealed himself to the Israelites and kept his covenant by bringing them into the Promised Land and giving them King David and the prophets. He then told them that Jesus, a descendant of King David, is the Savior sent to the world by God to establish a New Covenant. People believed the Good News when they heard Paul preach.

Acts 15:1-21

Council at
Jerusalem

In addition to Jews, many Gentiles wanted to follow the path of Jesus and were baptized. The Jewish people had been trained in the laws of Moses, but those who were Gentiles did not know those laws. The Jews began to argue whether the Gentile believers needed to also obey the Jewish laws in order to be saved. This was a serious question, so the apostles met to discuss it. This meeting, which we now call the Council of Jerusalem, took place around the year AD 50. Paul, Barnabas, Peter, James, and the other apostles prayed and discussed the kinds of laws Gentiles should follow after baptism. Peter believed that both Jews and Gentiles were saved by the grace of God through Jesus Christ. Before his crucifixion and resurrection, Jesus had given Peter authority, the "keys to the kingdom" (Matthew 16:19), to guide the Church. At the council, Peter practiced this authority by reminding the apostles that, *"we shall be saved through the grace of the Lord Jesus, just as they will"* (Acts 15:11). James, who was the bishop of Jerusalem, agreed and spoke in union with Peter. Therefore, the council determined that Gentiles could also be part of the kingdom of God and did not have to follow some of the specific laws of the Jews, such as circumcision. The Church has followed the model of the Jerusalem Council for bishops and priests to gather to clarify matters of faith under the guidance of the Holy Spirit. (The Church has had twenty-one councils in its history, the most recent one being the Second Vatican Council, or **Vatican II,** which took place in the 1960s.)

Nicene Creed

I believe in one, holy, catholic, and apostolic Church.

What do you think?

1. What is our pope's name, and how does he follow Jesus?

2. How do you think good rules are made?

3. How would you tell someone else about your faith?

So the word of the Lord grew
and prevailed mightily.
– Acts 19:20

All Are Welcome in the Church

Narrative Book: Acts
Supplemental Books: Paul's Letters (Epistles)

Bible Reading Checklist

- [ ] Acts **15**:36-41; **16**   Paul's second missionary journey

- [ ] Acts **17–18**:11; **19**:1-20   Paul continues his journeys

- [ ] Acts **21**:27-40; **22**; **26**:1-23   Paul's arrest and defense

- [ ] Acts **27–28**:10   Shipwreck on the way to Rome

- [ ] Acts **28**:11-31   Paul in Rome

- [ ] Optional: *Catechism of the Catholic Church 966–967*
  The Assumption of Mary

Paul's Second
Missionary Journey

Inspired by the Holy Spirit, Paul went on a second journey to spread the Good News of Jesus and to support the new churches that had already been formed. The apostle Barnabas went to the island of Cyprus, and Paul and Silas went to the southern region of Asia Minor. On the way, Paul had a vision of a man from Macedonia inviting him to preach the gospel in that region, so he went there to a city called Philippi, which is part of the country now known as Greece. In Philippi, a woman named Lydia listened to Paul speak about Jesus. Lydia was a merchant who sold purple cloth. Her heart was open to the Word of God, and she asked that she and everyone in her household be baptized.

In the town of Philippi, not everyone was happy with the preaching of Paul and Silas. When Paul cast out an evil spirit from a slave girl, the leaders of the city put them in prison because of the commotion it caused. Paul and Silas prayed and sang hymns to God while they were in jail. While they were praying, an earthquake shook the prison and all of the doors flew open. The jailer became very afraid that the prisoners would leave and he would be punished. But Paul and Silas did not leave, and the jailer became a believer in Jesus. After this, the city leaders realized that Paul and Silas were Roman citizens, so they released them. Paul continued to spread the news of the salvation of Jesus throughout the cities of Macedonia and Greece. In some communities, like Thessalonica, there was resistance to the gospel and Paul and his companions were seen as attempting to place Jesus as a rival to Caesar. In other towns, like Beroea, the people were ready to listen to the Word of God and more people began to follow. Despite arrests and persecution, the apostles continued to spread the Good News.

Paul continued his journey in Athens and then went on to Corinth. There, he stayed with Aquila and his wife, Priscilla, Jews who had been expelled from Rome. Aquila and Paul were both tentmakers and practiced their trade together. Priscilla and Aquila welcomed Christians into their home and helped to spread the gospel.

Acts 17–18:11; 19:1-20

Paul Continues
His Journeys

Paul returned to Antioch and then began a third journey to visit many of the regions where he had preached before. He based his work in the city of Ephesus. The Ephesians had been baptized and were trying to follow God, but they needed the additional strength of the Holy Spirit to live fully the gospel message. Paul laid his hands on them so they could receive the Holy Spirit. The Ephesians were then able to witness to the Word of God throughout Asia. Paul wrote letters of encouragement to the new churches in the towns he had left. Many of these letters are a part of the New Testament and can offer wisdom for us, too. These books of the Bible are known as the *epistles*, or letters, of Paul. When Paul wrote to the Philippians at Philippi, he reminded them to be humble, as Christ was humble, and to love others by serving their needs (Philippians 2:1-11). Paul encouraged the Thessalonians in Thessalonica to, *"Rejoice always, pray constantly, give thanks in all circumstances; for this is the will of God in Christ Jesus for you"* (1 Thessalonians 5:16-18). In his letter to the Corinthians, Paul wrote about the many gifts that are given to all of us by the Holy Spirit. Each of these gifts helps us to contribute in a special way to work for the one body of Christ. Even though our gifts are different, they are all necessary and fit together for the good of everyone (1 Corinthians 12:7-31).

Acts 21:27-40; 22; 26:1-23

Paul's
Arrest and Defense

After three years in Ephesus, Paul returned to Jerusalem, even though the disciples said that he would not be safe there. Just as Jesus knew of the suffering he would face when he entered Jerusalem on Palm Sunday, Paul accepted what might happen to him in Jerusalem as the will of God. As it was predicted, some Jews accused Paul of preaching that they no longer had to follow their Law, and they had him arrested in Jerusalem and put on trial. Then he was transferred to Caesarea, where the governors Felix and then Festus questioned him, followed by King Agrippa. Paul retold his story of growing up as a devout Jew and how he persecuted the first Christians. He talked about his conversion on the road to Damascus and his work for Jesus to proclaim light to the Jews and to the Gentiles. Since he was a Roman citizen, Paul appealed to Caesar for a fair trial, so he was taken by ship to Rome.

Acts 27–28:10

Shipwreck on the Way to Rome

The journey to Rome was long and difficult because it was late in the year and the seas were stormy. At one point the winds became so strong that everyone thought they would die, but Paul had a vision of Jesus, who told him he was destined to stand before Caesar and all on the ship would survive. The ship was blown by the storm to an island called Malta. Everyone jumped into the sea and swam to the island before the ship began to break up in the waves. The native people greeted them and helped them build a fire and find food. Suddenly, Paul was bitten by a snake but, miraculously, he did not die. Because of this miracle and Paul's preaching, many of the people of the island became believers in Jesus.

Acts 28:11-31

Paul in Rome

Paul and the ship's crew spent the winter on the island of Malta before setting sail on another ship. Eventually, Paul arrived in Rome, where he was received warmly by many fellow Christians. Caesar did not pursue any charges against him, so Paul freely preached the gospel in Rome, fulfilling the call of Jesus to go out to the ends of the earth to preach the gospel (Matthew 28:18-20). For two years, Paul was allowed to teach about Jesus.

The book of Acts ends here, but the gospel continued to be spread by the apostles. Eleven of the apostles, as well as Paul, were martyred for their faith. John was exiled to the island of Patmos, where he had the vision described in the book of Revelation, the last book of the Bible. Their message continues to spread throughout the world and through the Church and is now passed to our generation.

The book of Acts ends here, but the gospel continued to be spread by the apostles. Eleven of the apostles, as well as Paul, were martyred for their faith. John was exiled to the island of Patmos, where he had the vision described in the book of Revelation, the last book of the Bible. Their message continues to spread throughout the world and through the Church and is now passed to our generation.

Optional: *Catechism of the Catholic Church 966–967*

The Assumption of Mary

When her life on earth came to an end, the Blessed Virgin Mary's body and soul was assumed, or taken up, into heaven by God. We know that Mary was faithful to following God, and so her body was brought to heaven as one of the first fruits of the resurrection of her son, Jesus (1 Corinthians 15:20). Her **assumption** gives all Christians hope of what God has in store for them. Mary is a gift to the Church as our Mother and as our helper on the journey to heaven by her **intercession**.

Fourth Glorious Mystery
The Assumption of Mary into Heaven
(CCC 966)

> *There is neither Jew nor Greek, there is neither slave nor free, there is neither male nor female; for you are all one in Christ Jesus.*
>
> – Galatians 3:28

What do you think?

1. How could St. Paul suffer so much and yet be joyful?

2. In what ways do you keep in touch with your loved ones who live far away?

3. Can you say the Hail Mary? How does Mary help us?

Behold, I stand at the door and knock; if any one hears my voice and opens the door, I will come in to him and eat with him, and he with me.
– Revelation 3:20

Chapter Twenty-Four

The Kingdom of God Is Eternal

Narrative Book: Revelation

Bible Reading Checklist

☐	Revelation **1**; **3**:14-22	John's first vision; letters to the churches
☐	Revelation **4–5**	The sacrificed Lamb is worshiped in heaven
☐	Revelation **6–8**:1	The coming judgment and the sealed ones
☐	Revelation **12**:1-16; **19**:1-16	The vision of Mary; the Wedding Supper
☐	Revelation **20**:1-10; **21–22**	The Last Judgment

Introduction to
Revelation

The book of Revelation sheds light on several parts of our faith, including the Mass, Mary, and the Last Judgment. The word *revelation* means "to show." It is written in an **apocalyptic** style, which uses symbols and images to connect current and future events with biblical events. Revelation is the last book of the Bible, and it may be the most difficult to understand. However, it is important because it tells us how to truly worship God through what he revealed to the apostle John. By writing this book, John pulls back a veil to reveal the covenant Bridegroom, Jesus, and his beautiful bride, the Church. Revelation provides encouragement to the Church when it faces difficult times.

Revelation 1; 3:14-22
John's
First Vision

During the first century after Christ's death and resurrection, the Church was persecuted for its belief in Jesus as the Son of God. Many people were suffering and dying because it was not permitted to preach the gospel in some places. John was held prisoner on an island called Patmos. As John prayed on the Lord's Day, Sunday, he heard a voice and turned around to see one who was "*like a son of man*" (Daniel 7:13-14). His eyes glowed like fire and he was holding seven stars. He was dressed in the clothing of a Jewish high priest. It was Jesus, walking among seven golden lampstands.

When John saw that it was Jesus, he fell at his feet in adoration. Jesus told him not to be afraid; then he told John that the seven stars were the angels of seven churches, and the lampstands were those churches. Jesus instructed John to write seven letters, one to each church represented by the lampstands.

Letters
to the Churches

The letters to the seven churches encouraged them to remain faithful to God. They also told them to stop doing things that were wrong and to remember that God will give eternal life in heaven to all who believe in Jesus Christ.

One of the letters was to the church in the city of Laodicea. Jesus said that the people in that church were "lukewarm," meaning they were not cold or hot. Jesus went on to say that because they were neither cold nor hot, he was going to spit them out of his mouth. He meant that he wished for them to have strong enthusiasm for God instead of halfhearted faith. The people of Laodicea were wealthy and owned many nice things, but they were poor spiritually because they thought they didn't need Jesus. In this letter are the comforting words of Jesus, *"Behold, I stand at the door and knock; if any one hears my voice and opens the door, I will come in to him and eat with him, and he with me"* (Revelation 3:20). We experience a foretaste of this heavenly banquet when we share the Eucharistic meal together at Mass.

Revelation 4–5
The Sacrificed Lamb
Is Worshiped in Heaven

Jesus invited John to come up to heaven to experience what it is like. John entered through an open door and saw a room in which God was seated on a throne. All heaven was worshiping God with twenty-four elders, representing the twelve tribes of Israel and the twelve apostles. Around God were four living creatures that looked like a lion, an ox, a man, and an eagle, which Catholic Tradition says represent the four Gospel writers. The presence of four creatures also indicates that believers in God will come from all four corners of the earth (CCC 1137–1139). They were worshiping God, saying, *"Holy, holy, holy is the Lord God almighty ..."* (Revelation 4:8).

John looked at the right hand of God and saw that he held a scroll, rolled up and secured with seven seals. On the scroll were written words of sorrowful news to anyone who breaks the commandments. There was an angel who was calling out for someone worthy to break the seals of the scroll so that it could be read and the judgment carried out. No one was found worthy until they saw the "*Lamb standing, as though it had been slain"* (Revelation 5:6). Jesus is the Paschal (or Easter) Lamb, the one who was found to be without sin but was sacrificed so we could be saved, just as the lamb without blemish was sacrificed at the first Passover in Egypt to save the Israelites from the angel of death (Exodus 12). The living creatures, the elders, and countless voices began to worship God, proclaiming, *"Worthy is the lamb who was slain and takes away the sins of the world!"* (Revelation 5:6-13). Jesus is worthy to open the scroll because he obeyed God the Father completely and became the perfect sacrificial Lamb, who died on the Cross to take away our sins.

Revelation 6–8:1
The Coming Judgment
and the Sealed Ones

John saw Jesus open the seven seals one at a time. After he opened each seal, one of the four living creatures called, "Come forward," and there was a response each time. After the first seal was broken, a white horse and rider approached. The rider was carrying a bow and wore a crown like a king. This rider represents Jesus who would come as a powerful warrior and judge. The next three seals brought horses and riders of a different kind. They symbolized the many bad things that would happen in the world because of sin, like sickness, fighting, and death. The fifth seal brought the martyrs: people who were killed because of their faith in Jesus. The sixth seal brought a terrible earthquake, which represents the bad consequences of sin.

Before the seventh seal on the scroll was broken, a seal was placed on the foreheads of those who were faithful to God to protect them from the trials to come. These people came from all over the earth and were marked with a sign of faith, just as we receive the Holy Spirit in confirmation as a sign of our total belonging to Christ (CCC 2159, 1296). The breaking of the seventh seal was followed by silence; then a series of trials began, similar to those inflicted upon the Egyptians by the ten plagues as told in the book of Exodus.

Revelation 12:1-16; 19:1-16

The Vision of Mary

Another great sign was revealed to John—a woman in the sky! John went on to describe her as one who was clothed with the sun, with the moon under her feet, and a crown of twelve stars on her head, who was about to give birth. A huge red dragon wanted to devour her baby because he was destined to rule the world. As soon as the child was born, he was taken up to God and his throne. This woman is the Blessed Virgin Mary, who carried the child Jesus in her womb. Jesus is our Bread of Life, our High Priest, and the Word made flesh.

Fifth Glorious Mystery
The Coronation of Mary
(Revelation 12:1)

The vision reminds us of the Ark of the Covenant in the Old Testament, which carried manna (the saving food for the Israelites), Aaron's budding rod (symbolizing the high priest), and the stone tablets of the Ten Commandments (the Word of God) (Hebrews 9:4). Mary, as Queen of Heaven, is a sign of hope and comfort to all of God's faithful people as we make up his Church on earth (CCC 972).

The Wedding Supper

In John's vision, the multitudes in heaven were singing praises to God because a great wedding was taking place. The Marriage of the Lamb, who is Jesus, and his bride, the Church, had come. The bride had been given clothing of fine linen, bright and pure. This clothing signifies the righteous deeds of the saints. God invites each of us to join him for a special banquet in the Marriage Supper of the Lamb. We get a foretaste of this feast when we celebrate the Eucharist, which offers food for our journey until we can celebrate the eternal banquet with God in heaven (CCC 1244). The angel told John to write this down, *"Blessed are those who are invited to the marriage supper of the Lamb"* (Revelation 19:9). Each time that we celebrate Mass, it is with the communion of saints, which is the unity of all saints and believers on earth and in heaven who form one, holy, catholic, and apostolic Church (CCC 960–962).

Revelation 20:1-10; 21–22

The Last Judgment

The heavenly throne room is the heart of the book of Revelation, because it is there that John witnesses not only the end of our earthly journey but also the beginning of what is to come. The Last Judgment is God's final victory over sin and death. As John continues to watch, he sees Satan thrown into the abyss of hell. Then, all the saints and martyrs are resurrected and reign with Christ. Everyone whose name is found written in the book of life will joyfully live forever in heaven with Christ. Anyone whose name is not found

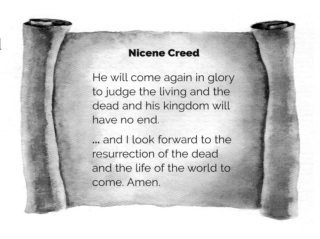

Nicene Creed

He will come again in glory to judge the living and the dead and his kingdom will have no end.

... and I look forward to the resurrection of the dead and the life of the world to come. Amen.

in the book of life will be thrown into the lake of fire (John 5:26-29). Then John saw a beautiful vision of heaven. He saw a river flowing from the throne of God and of the Lamb. The springs were full of life-giving water, which is God's grace, and the Tree of Life was growing on the side of the river. Nothing sinful was there nor will ever be there, only goodness. God and the Lamb, Jesus, are on the throne. The servants will worship him there and God's name will be on their foreheads. There will not be any need for a lamp or sun, because God will be their light and he will reign forever.

The Bible ends with the word *Amen,* which means "so be it" or "yes, it is so."

This is the Good News that God wanted to share with us since the beginning of time—God is love! The story of salvation is our invitation to a personal relationship with Jesus as part of the Church, his bride. Accepting Jesus' invitation allows him to touch our hearts in an intimate embrace. The door to heaven has opened. You are invited. Will you eat at the table with the Lamb?

What do you think?

1. Have you ever imagined that there are angels and saints worshiping at Mass with you?

2. If Jesus knocked on your door, would you open the door and welcome him in? What would you say to him?

3. How do you create a holy heart for worshiping God?

Afterword
The Story Continues with You

Congratulations! You have read the story of salvation. Hopefully, you understand the incredible love God has for you as shown through his Son, Jesus Christ, and in his Church. Just as he did with his disciples in the New Testament, Jesus Christ is still working in the lives of people of every generation all around the world. We are now living in the period of "the Church," which is the final stage before Jesus comes again in glory to judge the living and the dead.

In the box below is the basic summary of the story of salvation that you can share with others.

- God loves you and wants a relationship with you (John 3:16).
- Sin has broken our relationship with God (Genesis 3).
- Jesus Christ died to pay the penalty for your sins (Romans 5:8).
- Believe in the gospel (John 14:6-7; John 11:25-27).
- Repent, be baptized, and receive the Holy Spirit (Acts 2:38).
- Live in Christ by keeping his commandments and remaining in communion with his body, the Church (Matthew 5:3-9).
- Go and make disciples of Christ (Matthew 28:19-20).

The following steps are necessary for being part of the one, holy, catholic, and apostolic Church:

1. **Receive the sacrament of baptism:** To become a member of the Church, it is necessary to be baptized. Baptism is the sacrament that brings us from a life of sin to a life of holiness. (You were probably baptized as an infant.) After baptism, the sacraments of confirmation and Eucharist complete your initiation into the Church.

   Baptism … now saves you, not as a removal of dirt from the body but as an appeal to God for a clear conscience, through the resurrection of Jesus Christ, who has gone into heaven and is at the right hand of God, with angels, authorities, and powers subject to him. – 1 Peter 3:21-22

2. **Celebrate the sacrament of reconciliation:** We sometimes sin against God and others by doing what is wrong, so God has provided the sacrament of reconciliation—also called *confession*—to bring us back to the state of grace we received when we were baptized.

   If we confess our sins, he is faithful and just, and will forgive our sins and cleanse us from all unrighteousness. – **1 John 1:9**

3. **Enter into the New Covenant through the Holy Eucharist:** Jesus has invited us into communion with him in the Eucharist, where he shares his very Body and Blood with those who are part of his Church. By receiving Jesus in the Holy Eucharist, we acknowledge Jesus as Lord and we draw strength to live a holy life.

   And he took bread, and when he had given thanks he broke it and gave it to them, saying, "This is my body which is given for you. Do this in remembrance of me." And likewise the cup after supper, saying, "This cup which is poured out for you is the new covenant in my blood." – **Luke 22:19-20**

4. **Pray:** To communicate with God, we need to speak and listen to him. A part of every day should be spent talking with God. There are books with prayers you can read, or you can simply have a conversation with him since he is your Father and a friend.

   Have no anxiety about anything, but in everything by prayer and supplication with thanksgiving let your requests be made known to God. – **Philippians 4:6**

5. **Live a life of charity:** To show others that you love Jesus, you need to live a life of charity, imitating the way Jesus and Mary lived on earth. They were truly loving and generous, and all that they did was to glorify God and to help other people. The life of charity includes living the virtues of faith, hope, and love, as well as prudence, temperance, fortitude, and justice (CCC 1803–1829).

   A new commandment I give to you, that you love one another; even as I have loved you, that you also love one another. By this all men will know that you are my disciples, if you have love for one another. – **John 13:34-35**

6. **Teach others the story:** Continue to grow in your understanding of the Church's teachings through reading the Bible, the *Catechism of the Catholic Church,* and the writings of the popes and saints. With this knowledge and the power of the Holy Spirit, you can share with anyone how they can be part of the story, too!

   Go therefore and make disciples of all nations, baptizing them in the name of the Father and of the Son and of the Holy Spirit, teaching them to observe all that I have commanded you; and lo, I am with you always, to the close of the age." – **Matthew 28:19-20**

Glossary

AD – abbreviation of the Latin phrase *in anno Domini*, meaning "in the year of the Lord"; used with years following the birth of Jesus.

Apocalyptic – a literary style in the Bible that uses symbolic terms and imagery to describe past, present, and future events. The book of Revelation and sections of Daniel are examples of apocalyptic literature in the Bible.

Apostle – from a Greek word meaning "one who is sent"; the apostles were chosen by Jesus to go out and preach the gospel. This includes the original group of twelve chosen by Jesus, as well as Paul and Barnabas.

Archaeologists – scientists who study the remains of buildings, artifacts, and bones from ancient times to learn about previous cultures.

Ark of the Covenant – also called the "Ark of God" or "Ark of the LORD"; built according to the instructions given by God to Moses; the gold-covered, wooden chest that held the Ten Commandments, Aaron's budding rod, and manna; carried by Levites on two poles during the time of the Tabernacle and later permanently placed in the "Holy of Holies" of the Temple in Jerusalem.

Asherah – a female fertility goddess worshiped by the Canaanites usually represented in the form of a wooden pole.

Assumption, the – the bodily "taking up" of Mary into heaven at the end of her earthly life. In the words of Pope Pius XII when he defined this dogma in 1950, "Having completed the course of her earthly life, [Mary] was assumed body and soul into heavenly glory" *(Munificentissimus Deus)*.

Assyria – a world power during the Divided Kingdom period of Bible history, located north of Israel in the region of Mesopotamia. The Assyrian army defeated the Northern Kingdom of Israel and took them into exile in 722 BC.

Assyrians – the people of Assyria.

Ba'al – a male Canaanite deity.

Babylon – a world power in Mesopotamia. The Babylonian army conquered Judah in 587 BC.

Babylonians – people of the Babylonian Empire.

Baptism – from a Greek work meaning "to immerse." Jesus commanded the apostles to "teach all nations, baptizing them in the name of the Father and of the Son and of the Holy Spirit" (Matthew 28:19). The baptism of John was a sign of repentance (Matthew 3:11) that foreshadowed the sacrament of baptism instituted by Christ.

BC – an abbreviation for "before Christ"; used with years before the birth of Jesus.

Book of the Law of Moses – the first five books of the Bible—Genesis, Exodus, Leviticus, Numbers, and Deuteronomy—which were once written on a single scroll; also called the Pentateuch ("five books"), the Torah, the Book of the Law, or the Law of Moses.

Canaan – the land promised to Abraham as an inheritance; also called the "Levant," the "Promised Land," "Israel," and, in more recent times, "Palestine."

Census – an official recording of the people living in a particular geographical region.

Centurion – a Roman army officer who commanded a hundred soldiers.

Cherubim – a Hebrew word for "angels." After God cast Adam and Eve out of the Garden of Eden, he placed cherubim to guard it (Genesis 3:24).

Christ – from a Greek word meaning "anointed one" (Matthew 16:16; CCC 453); translation of the Hebrew word *Messiah*.

Christians – followers of Jesus Christ, who have been baptized in his name.

Church – in the New Testament, the Greek word *ekklesia* ("to call out of") is used to refer to the universal assembly of believers in Jesus. The Church was established by Christ, and its members include all baptized Christians who profess the same faith under the authority of Jesus Christ, the Church's "invisible head," and the pope, its "visible head."

Circumcision – a sign of God's covenant with the Jewish people.

Covenant – an agreement between God and one or more people. Usually involves the swearing of an oath. (See "Six Covenants Established in the Bible" on page 190.)

Deacons – men of good reputation chosen by the apostles to help serve the Church, especially the poor and widowed. Today, deacons are ordained to assist bishops and priests in their ministry, by performing baptisms, officiating at marriages, assisting at Mass (particularly by reading the Gospel and preaching), and bringing Communion to those who are ill, among other duties.

Dead Sea Scrolls – a collection of scrolls written between the third century BC and the first century AD, discovered hidden in caves around the Dead Sea between 1946 and 1956; these scrolls contain portions of nearly every book of the Old Testament (except Esther).

Disciples – followers of Jesus.

Egypt – a world power in the ancient world in northern Africa, whose rule extended at times all the way north to Babylon. The seat of power, ruled by a Pharaoh, worshiped as though he were a god, was located along the Nile River Delta. Egypt was a world power from the Early World period of Bible history to the Divided Kingdom period of Bible history.

Emmanuel – a biblical name that means "God with us." In the Old Testament, the prophet Isaiah predicted the birth of Jesus with his words, "Behold, a young woman shall conceive and bear a son, and shall call his name Immanuel" (Isaiah 7). In the New Testament, an angel of the Lord appears to Joseph, telling him his son will fulfill this prophecy (Matthew 1:23).

Ethiopia – a country southeast of Egypt, also referred to as "Cush" in the Bible.

Eucharist – one of the seven sacraments of the Church. (See "The Seven Sacraments" on page 194.)

Eunuch – a male who is unable to produce children, often employed to protect women of status; such as the Ethiopian eunuch in Acts 8 who guarded the queen of Ethiopia.

Feast of Booths – also called "Sukkoth" or "Tabernacles," one of the three pilgrimage festivals required by Jewish law to be celebrated every year. In Jesus' time, this fall festival was celebrated in Jerusalem. Families built booths or tents and lived in them for the week to remind them that their forefathers wandered in the wilderness (Leviticus 23:33-36).

Feast of Passover – also called "Pesach," one of the three pilgrimage festivals required by Jewish law to be celebrated every year. In Jesus' time, this spring festival was celebrated in Jerusalem, where each family or group of families sacrificed a lamb and ate it with a meal that recalled the first Passover (Exodus

12:1-20), when God delivered them from Egypt. During this festival, Jesus instituted the Eucharist at the Last Supper during the Passover meal. Then he suffered, died, and rose from the dead within the eight days of the Feast of the Passover.

Feast of Pentecost – also called "Shavuot" or the "Feast of the Weeks," one of the three pilgrimage festivals required by Jewish law to be celebrated every year. In Jesus' time, this summer festival occurred fifty days after Passover and was celebrated in Jerusalem. This feast commemorates the giving of the Torah, the five books of Moses, to Moses on Mount Sinai. For the Catholic Church, Pentecost commemorates the birthday of the Church through the outpouring of the Holy Spirit on the apostles.

Feast of Unleavened Bread – this feast is combined with the Feast of Passover. During this weeklong festival, all leavened food was removed from a Jewish home to remind them how they left Egypt in haste (Exodus 12:18-20).

Gamaliel – a prominent rabbi from the time of Jesus, who was a member of the Jewish Council, or Sanhedrin, and was somewhat favorable toward the apostles.

Gentile – a non-Jewish person.

Hanukkah – also called the "Festival of Lights" or the "Feast of Dedication." It is an eight-day Jewish holiday started at the time of the Maccabean Revolt to commemorate the rededication of the Temple. Jesus attended this feast in Jerusalem (John 10:22-31) and told the Jewish leadership that he and his Father are one. They tried to stone him for saying that.

Hasmoneans – the dynasty of the Maccabean family that ruled from the time of the Maccabees until they were conquered by Herod the Great during the Maccabean Revolt period of Bible history.

Hellenism – the adoption of ancient Greek culture, language, art, and worship.

I AM WHO I AM – the holy name of God, which was first spoken to Moses. "I AM WHO I AM" is the English translation of the four-letter Hebrew word YHWH (commonly pronounced as "Yahweh") In traditional Judaism, this name is considered too holy to be spoken. Throughout the Old Testament, the Hebrew word *Adonai* ("LORD") is substituted for YHWH as a sign of reverence.

Incarnate – the word describing the event of God the Father's Son, while remaining God, becoming fully a human being. Jesus Christ is true God and true man. In him there is a perfect union of divine nature and human nature in a divine Person (CCC 464).

Inspired – in the context of Scripture, it means "God breathed." Under the inspiration of the Holy Spirit, the human authors of the Bible—freely using their own intellect and abilities—wrote down "the truth which God, for the sake of our salvation, wished to see confided to the Sacred Scripture" (CCC 107); and so, their words are the words of God.

Intercession – a type of prayer in which we place the needs of others before God. When someone says, "I'll pray for you," they are offering to be intercessors. When we bring our requests to Our Lady, the saints, and our guardian angels, they become our intercessors; they pray to God on behalf of those on earth in the same way that Jesus prays to the Father for us (CCC 2635).

Ishmaelite – a descendant of Ishmael, son of Abraham and the slave woman Hagar, the older half-brother of Isaac. Ishmael was sent away with his mother to live in Egypt after Isaac was born because Ishmael was not the child promised to Abraham and Sarah by God. (Genesis 16; 21:1-22).

Israelite – a descendant of the patriarch Jacob, also known as "Israel." Other common names used in the Bible for the Israelites are "Hebrews" or "children of Israel."

Jerusalem – the capital of Israel, located in Judah. Also called the "Holy City" because that is where King Solomon built the Temple. In the time of Abraham, the city was known as "Salem." In the time of David, it was occupied by the Jebusites, but David conquered it, and it became his capital.

Jew – a person who is a descendant from the tribe of Judah. After the Exile period of Bible history, those who returned to Jerusalem were called "Jews." Jesus was born of this lineage.

Judea – the geographic region where the tribe of Judah settled after the conquest of Canaan. It is the hilly region of Israel between the Mediterranean Sea and the Dead Sea. At the time of Jesus, this area was a province of Rome.

Lebanon – the nation to the north of Israel, or Canaan, known for its cedar forests.

Lepers – people who contracted the disease of leprosy were considered "unclean" according to the Law of Moses and had to live outside of the camp or city in a group by themselves.

Maccabees – a family group of Jews that revolted against the Seleucid king Antiochus Epiphanies. The priest Mattathias first refused to break the Law of Moses. He had several sons that were also involved in what became known as the "Maccabean Revolt." Judas Maccabeus was the most prominent son and had the nickname of the "hammer."

Manger – a feeding trough for animals. In biblical times, a manger was usually made from stone or wood.

Manna – the heavenly food provided by God to sustain the Israelites during the Desert Wanderings period. It was white, sweet, and could be made into cakes. After the Israelites entered the Promised Land, manna was no longer provided; however, one jar of it was saved in the Ark of the Covenant.

Martyr – someone who gives his or her life to defend his or her faith. They may be killed outright or caused to die by other circumstances related to defending their faith. "Martyr" comes from the Greek word meaning "witness." For Christians, a martyr is someone who is killed for defending their belief in Jesus.

Megiddo – an ancient city in northern Israel that overlooked and defended a trade route passing from Egypt to Mesopotamia. Many battles were fought at Megiddo between the various ancient powers. The valley below this city, Armageddon, is said to be the place of the last earthly battle (Revelation 16:12-16). Megiddo is currently an archeological site.

Messiah – this word means "anointed one" in Hebrew; the one who would deliver the Jewish people from oppression. Jesus is understood in Christianity to be the Messiah predicted in the Old Testament. The word *Christ* is from the Greek word for *Messiah*.

Monastery – usually a place of residence for monks or nuns who are living in seclusion under religious vow.

Moriah – a mountain range in the area of Judah that runs through Jerusalem, where Abraham offers Isaac. It is believed that the location of the sacrifice of Abraham is where the Temple Mount was built in Jerusalem. The name "Zion" is also used for this mountainous area of Jerusalem.

Mount Sinai – an important mountain in the Bible, located in the wilderness between Egypt and the Promised Land. The Israelites camped at this mountain after leaving Egypt, and Moses received the Ten Commandments there. It was also the location of the burning bush and where Elijah hears the "still small voice" of God (1 Kings 19:8-14). Sinai is also called Mount Horeb, "the mountain of God," where Moses brought water from the rock. The exact location of Mount Sinai is unknown, but the traditional site near St. Catherine's Monastery is a place of pilgrimage and is visited by thousands every year.

Mythological – based on myths or fables.

Nazirite – a person who has taken a special vow to be set apart for God's service. A sign of the vow is that they do not cut their hair, they do not consume anything made from grapes, and they do not touch the deceased.

Original Sin – due to the sin of our first parents (Adam and Eve), we inherit the "stain" of original sin, meaning we are born in a "state of sin" and need redemption. Baptism purifies us from original sin; it brings us into the life of grace and makes us members of the Church. Mary was the only human person who was conceived and born without original sin, by a unique ("singular") grace of God, so that she would be prepared to be the mother of the God-man, Jesus (CCC 490–493).

Passion, the – refers to the period of time of suffering from Jesus' agony in the Garden of Gethsemane through his arrest, trial, and crucifixion.

Persecution – intentional harassment or abuse of a person or group of people by another person or group, often due to a conflict in religious belief or practice.

Persia – a world power during the Exile period of Bible history. Persia conquered Babylon and was later conquered by Greece in 334 BC. Much of the Persian Empire is now the modern country of Iran.

Pharisees – members of a Jewish religious group that strictly followed the laws of Moses. What they believed was good, but the way they lived their beliefs was not, according to Jesus (Matthew 23:1-7).

Plagues – a series of debilitating catastrophes that fell upon the Egyptians because of the refusal of Pharaoh to let the Israelites go and worship God. There were ten plagues in all, the last being the death of the firstborn.

Pope – the bishop of Rome. As the visible head of the Church, he is also called the "Vicar of Christ" and the "Roman Pontiff." He is traditionally referred to as the "Holy Father" or "His Holiness." The first pope was the apostle St. Peter, followed by 265 successors down to Pope Francis, the 266th pope.

Prodigal – someone who is wasteful in spending; the term has come to mean "wayward" in describing the son who is welcomed back by his father in Jesus' parable of the Prodigal Son.

Promised Land – the territory that God promised to give Abraham. Other terms for the general geographical area are "Israel," "Canaan," the "Levant," and "Palestine."

Prophets – persons chosen by God to proclaim the will of God and call people to live according to the covenant. Prophets sometimes tell what can happen in the future. In biblical times, they often played an important role as inspired advisors to kings. Besides prophets who spoke for God, there are also false prophets, such as the prophets involved in the worship of Ba'al.

Purim – a Jewish festival that commemorates Queen Esther for saving the Jewish people from extermination during the Exile period of Bible history.

Repentance – sorrow for having done something wrong along with the desire to amend one's life and do right in the future.

Sabbath – the seventh day of Creation when God rested. God required people to rest from their labors on the seventh day. Since the resurrection of Jesus was on the first day of the week, the Church sets aside Sunday as a special day of rest. Sunday is also called the "Lord's Day," referring to the Resurrection.

Sacrament – a sacred sign instituted by God to give grace. The seven sacraments were given to us by Jesus himself to celebrate and be drawn into a closer relationship with God himself. (See "The Seven Sacraments" on page194.)

Sadducees – members of a Jewish group at the time of Jesus that did not believe in the resurrection of the dead or the existence of spirits. They also did not believe in Jewish oral tradition, and they only accepted the written Law as binding on Jews. They were often at odds with the Pharisees.

Samaritans – people who lived in the area of Samaria, in the area given to the tribe of Ephraim. At the time of Christ, the people who lived there were not considered Jews, but their religious worship was similar. The Samaritans were descendants of the Northern Kingdom of Israel mixed with people from five nations brought to occupy the area of Samaria during the Exile period of Bible history.

Scribes – Jewish religious leaders who were experts in the Law and who helped hand on the traditions of Judaism.

Son of Man – a biblical expression that was used by the LORD when he spoke to the prophet Ezekiel. It also refers to an important person in Daniel's vision (Daniel 7:12-13), one who would stand before God and have dominion over all things for all time. Jesus called himself the Son of Man, showing that he was the fulfillment of Daniel's prophecy.

Swaddling clothes – strips of cloth used to wrap a baby.

Synagogue – a building used for Jewish worship and study. Jesus read from the Bible in the synagogue in Nazareth and taught at many synagogues around the Sea of Galilee. On their journeys, the apostles would stop at synagogues to teach about Jesus.

Tabernacle – a portable tent used for worship that housed the Ark of the Covenant. This colorful tent was hand-crafted by the Israelites during the time of the Desert Wanderings using the instructions that Moses received from God on Mount Sinai. The tribe of Levi was in charge of the Tabernacle and its furnishings, and the Levites transported the Tabernacle when the Israelite camp moved. This structure was used for worship until the first Temple was built in Jerusalem by King Solomon. Also referred to as the "Tent of Meeting," the "Dwelling," or the "Sanctuary."

Trinity – The Blessed Trinity is the central mystery of the Christian Faith (see CCC 234), the belief that the Father, the Son, and the Holy Spirit, three distinct Persons, are one God and share in a single divine nature.

Unclean spirits – angels that have fallen and do the work of the devil; also called "evil spirits" or "demons."

Vatican II – also known as the "Second Vatican Council." One of the twenty-one *ecumenical councils* held in the history of the Church, Vatican II met from 1962 to 1965. An ecumenical council is a gathering of the bishops of the Church, called together (or at least approved) by the pope. An important document issued by Vatican II is *Dei Verbum* ("The Word of God"), which discusses divine revelation as it is contained in the Bible and Sacred Tradition and how this revelation is handed on to every generation.

Veil of the Temple – a thick woven curtain that separated the Holy of Holies—the innermost room of the Temple that contained the Ark of the Covenant—from the "Holy Place," the outer room. This veil was made of heavy red and purple yarn and embroidered with cherubim angels. During Christ's crucifixion, the veil being torn in two signified that Jewish Temple worship was being replaced by the new Temple, the body of Christ, the Church, which would include all peoples.

Womb – a place in a woman's body where babies grow before birth; the "uterus."

Zion – a term used to mean the mountain of the LORD or the place where God is present. The holy city of Jerusalem is also called "Zion."

Supplemental Books of the Bible

- Leviticus
- Deuteronomy
- Ruth
- 1 Chronicles
- 2 Chronicles
- Tobit
- Judith
- Esther
- Job
- Psalms
- Proverbs
- Ecclesiastes
- Song of Solomon
- Wisdom of Solomon

- Sirach
- Isaiah
- Jeremiah
- Lamentations
- Baruch
- Ezekiel
- Daniel
- Hosea
- Joel
- Amos
- Obadiah
- Jonah
- Micah
- Nahum
- Habakkuk
- Zephaniah

- Haggai
- Zechariah
- Malachi
- 2 Maccabees
- Matthew
- Mark
- John
- Romans
- 1 Corinthians
- 2 Corinthians
- Galatians
- Ephesians
- Philippians
- Colossians
- 1 Thessalonians
- 2 Thessalonians

- 1 Timothy
- 2 Timothy
- Titus
- Philemon
- Hebrews
- James
- 1 Peter
- 2 Peter
- 1 John
- 2 John
- 3 John
- Jude
- Revelation

Appendices
The Six Covenants Established in the Bible

A covenant in the Bible is an agreement between God and an individual or group. Everyone who is part of the covenant makes a solemn promise to agree to its terms and swears an oath to be faithful to it. Both parties agree to keep their promise, even if this means suffering or dying. God's relationship with us has developed through a progression of six covenants described in the Bible. The progression began with two people—Adam and Eve—and has grown to include all people who are members of the Church.

The First Covenant:
One Holy Couple

Covenant with Adam and Eve

God established his first covenant with Adam and Eve, the first man and woman who were united in marriage, *One Holy Couple*. From their union, the world would be blessed. The Sabbath day of rest was given to Adam and Eve as a sign to rest from their labor and to commune with God. The covenant of marriage and the sign of the Sabbath are linked with Creation. It is fitting that marriage is linked with Creation, as it is here that new life begins. Marriage is the foundation of a family unit. (Genesis 1–3; found in *Storybook* Chapter Two.)

The Second Covenant:
One Holy Family

Covenant with Noah and his family

After the great Flood, Noah and his family came out of the ark and saw a rainbow in the sky. This rainbow was given by God as the sign of the second covenant he made with his people. God promised Noah that he would never again destroy the whole earth with a flood. This covenant with Noah and his family is *One Holy Family*. They would learn how to love and obey God as they again filled the earth with children and grandchildren. (Genesis 9; found in *Storybook* Chapter Three.)

The Third Covenant:
One Holy Tribe

Covenant with Abraham

God made a covenant with Abram, promising him that he would have as many descendants as there are stars in the sky. Abram was ninety-nine years old, yet miraculously, this promise came true with the birth of Isaac. The third covenant that God made with his people is *One Holy Tribe*. God also promised to give Abram land and a royal dynasty. As a sign of this covenant, God changed Abram's name to Abraham. Abraham promised to dedicate to God through circumcision all his male children and grandchildren and all the following generations and to obey all of God's laws. Circumcision is the sign of the covenant. (Genesis 15, 17, 22; found in *Storybook* Chapter Four.)

The Fourth Covenant:
One Holy Nation

Covenant with Moses

After God delivered the Israelites from the bondage of Egypt through the Passover, the Israelites stood at the foot of Mount Sinai, where Moses sacrificed young bulls and sprinkled some of the blood on the people saying, "This is the blood of the covenant which the LORD has made with you." God promised to make them a mighty nation of priests, *One Holy Nation*. The people agreed to obey all that the LORD had commanded them to do. As a sign of this covenant, God gave Moses two tablets of stone with the Ten Commandments written on them. All the Israelites except for the tribe of Levi broke this covenant by worshiping an idol; consequently, only Levites served as priests. God still blessed the Israelites as a nation. (Exodus 24; Deuteronomy 29; found in *Storybook* Chapter Seven.)

The Fifth Covenant:
One Holy Kingdom

Covenant with David

God made a covenant with King David, promising that he would give him a son who would build a house for the LORD and establish a kingdom for all the people. God promised that David's kingdom, *One Holy Kingdom,* would last forever and that he would not take his steadfast love away from him. The sign of this covenant is the Temple in Jerusalem, which was built by David's son Solomon. Jesus is the promised Messiah who came from David's royal line. (2 Samuel 7:11-15; found in *Storybook* Chapter Twelve.)

The Sixth Covenant:
One Holy Church

New Covenant with Christ

Jesus ushered in the New Covenant by dying on the Cross for our sins, then rising again and ascending into heaven. He was the perfect sacrifice who could at last break the power of death and sin over people. The Holy Eucharist is the eternal memorial of the New Covenant. The New Covenant family of God is the body of Christ, the Church, *One Holy Church,* who by the power of the Holy Spirit can live the will of Christ here on earth. While all people who are baptized into Christ have a share in the Church, full communion involves sharing the bonds of faith, sacraments, and pastoral governance found in the teachings of the Catholic Church. (Matthew 16:18; Luke 22:1-23; found in *Storybook* Chapter Twenty.)

Nicene Creed

The Nicene Creed is a confession of faith that was issued by the First Council of Nicaea in AD 325. It is recited at every Sunday Mass and on solemn feasts. Excerpts from the Nicene Creed have been placed into this *Storybook* at certain points to help children better understand what they recite each week at Mass. The locations of these are noted below in parentheses.

I believe in one God, the Father almighty, maker of heaven and earth, of all things visible and invisible. (Chapter Two)

I believe in one Lord Jesus Christ, the Only Begotten Son of God, born of the Father before all ages. God from God, Light from Light, true God from true God, begotten, not made, consubstantial with the Father; through him all things were made. (Chapter Two)

For us men and for our salvation he came down from heaven, (bow) and by the Holy Spirit was incarnate of the Virgin Mary, and became man. (Chapter Eighteen)

For our sake he was crucified under Pontius Pilate, he suffered death and was buried, and rose again on the third day in accordance with the Scriptures. He ascended into heaven and is seated at the right hand of the Father. (Chapter Twenty)

He will come again in glory to judge the living and the dead and his kingdom will have no end. (Chapter Twenty-Four)

I believe in the Holy Spirit, the Lord, the giver of life, who proceeds from the Father and the Son, who with the Father and the Son is adored and glorified, who has spoken through the prophets. (Chapter Twenty-One)

I believe in one, holy, catholic, and apostolic Church. (Chapter Twenty-Two)

I confess one baptism for the forgiveness of sins (Chapter Twenty-One) *and I look forward to the resurrection of the dead and the life of the world to come. Amen.* (Chapter Twenty-Four)

The Seven Sacraments

The seven sacraments have been given to us by Jesus so that we can experience God's presence and his saving grace. Each sacrament is an outward sign of a greater, inward reality that gives us God's grace to become closer to him and to do his work on earth.

Sacraments of Initiation

The three sacraments that provide the foundation for Christian life.

1. Baptism

Baptism is birth into new life in Christ (CCC 1277); the first sacrament of initiation—that is, the first step on our journey in the Faith. Baptism forgives sins and makes us members of the Church.

> ***Signs and words:*** Water is poured on our heads (or we are immersed in it), as the words, "I baptize you in the name of the Father, and of the Son, and of the Holy Spirit," are spoken by the priest or deacon.

> ***Sacramental grace:*** Original sin—and, if the person being baptized is beyond the age of reason—and personal sins are forgiven, and we become a member of the Church.

> ***Frequency:*** Once. It must be received before any other sacrament.

> ***Bible verses:*** Matthew 28:19-20; John 3:3, 22; 4:1-2; Acts 2:38.

2. Confirmation

In confirmation, we receive an outpouring of the Holy Spirit in order to be a stronger member of the Church and a witness of faith (CCC 1316). This is one of the three sacraments of initiation.

> ***Signs and words:*** A bishop anoints our foreheads with sacred oil (chrism) and says the words, "Be sealed with the Gift of the Holy Spirit" (CCC 1320).

> ***Sacramental grace:*** We are strengthened by the Holy Spirit and become full members of the Church.

Frequency: Once. (In the United States, confirmation is usually received in middle school, but it may be received in high school in some dioceses. Adults converting to the Faith also receive confirmation as part of the Rite of Christian Initiation of Adults process.)

Bible verses: John 20:22; Acts 2:4, 8:14-17, 19:6; 2 Corinthians 1:21-22 (CCC 1296), 2 Corinthians 2:15 (CCC 1294).

3. The Holy Eucharist

The Eucharist is the real Body, Blood, Soul, and Divinity of Christ in the form of bread and wine (CCC 1374). It is one of the three sacraments of initiation, the one in which we receive Christ himself and are united with all Catholics on earth and in heaven (CCC 1326). Jesus gave us the Eucharist at the Last Supper with the same words used by the priest during the Liturgy of the Eucharist at Mass.

Signs and words: We eat and drink what appears to be bread and wine, which have changed into the Body and Blood of Christ through the consecration at Mass. The priest, deacon, or extraordinary minister holds up the host (or cup) and says, "The Body (or Blood) of Christ," and we reply, "Amen."

Sacramental grace: We are spiritually nourished by Christ's Body and Blood, and we are united "in communion" with Christ and all members of the Church.

Frequency: If we are in the state of grace, we are encouraged to receive Communion whenever we attend Mass (CCC 1388). At minimum, a Catholic should receive the Eucharist at least once a year—if possible, during the Easter season (CCC 1389).

Bible verses: Matthew 26:26-29; Mark 14:22-25; Luke 22:14-20; John 6:48-58; Acts 20:7.

Sacraments of Healing

4. Reconciliation (also called Penance or Confession)

In the sacrament of reconciliation, we receive God's forgiveness for our sins. We confess our sins and express sorrow over them. We perform an act of penance and acknowledge the desire to avoid sin in the future. Broken relationships are healed through confession.

Signs and words: We confess our sins to a priest, and we resolve to perform the penance for them given to us by him. The priest, acting with the authority given to him by Christ himself through his ordination, administers God's forgiveness with the words of absolution: "I absolve you from your sins in the name of the Father, and of the Son, and of the Holy Spirit."

Sacramental grace: Our sins are forgiven, and we are reconciled with God and the Church.

Frequency: Reconciliation may be received as often as we need it throughout our lives, but we are required to confess any mortal sins before receiving Communion. Some people go to confession every week as an act of devotion to receive God's grace and be strengthened in virtue, even though they may have only venial sins to confess. The Church teaches we must go to confession at least once a year during Lent, in preparation for Easter.

Bible verses: Matthew 16:19, 18:18; John 20:22-23; James 5:16.

5. Anointing of the Sick

A priest anoints the forehead and hands of the sick person with blessed oil, praying for his or her physical and spiritual healing.

Signs and words: Blessed oil is used to anoint the forehead and hands of a sick person with the prayer, "Through this holy anointing may the Lord in his love and mercy help you with the grace of the Holy Spirit. May the Lord who frees you from sin save you and raise you up."

Sacramental grace: The sick person is strengthened in his or her time of illness and prepared to enter eternal life.

Frequency: Anointing of the sick may be received whenever we are seriously ill.

Bible verses: Mark 6:7-13; Luke 9:2; James 5:14-16.

Sacraments of Service

6. Holy Orders

To continue the ministry Jesus gave to the first apostles, the sacrament of holy orders is given to men who are called to serve his people as deacons, priests, or bishops.

Signs and words: A bishop lays his hands upon the head of the man being ordained and says a special prayer of consecration, asking God to send the Holy Spirit to help the new priest or deacon to perform the duties of his office (CCC 1573).

Sacramental grace: Through ordination, deacons, priests, and bishops are given a special sacramental "seal" (or mark) that gives them the power to act with the authority of Jesus himself.

Frequency: A man can only be ordained once to each of the three levels (or "degrees") of holy orders—deacon, priest, and bishop. This sacrament may only be received by a baptized man (CCC 1598).

Bible verses: Mark 3:13-19; Luke 5:10-11; John 20:21-23; Acts 6:6; 1 Timothy 4:14, 5:22; 2 Timothy 1:6.

7. Matrimony (or Marriage)

The sacrament of matrimony, or marriage, is a public sign of the loving union of a man and a woman for life, celebrated in a Mass. The man and woman give themselves to each other and remain open to having children (CCC 1601).

Signs and words: A husband and wife marry each other when they profess their vows in the presence of a priest or deacon and two other witnesses.

Sacramental grace: The couple is united to each other, and they become "one flesh." They receive God's grace to love each other and to welcome and educate their children. The sacrament of marriage may only be received by two baptized Christians.

Frequency: Once, unless one of the spouses dies or the marriage is declared invalid by the Church. When a spouse dies, the other spouse is free to marry.

Bible verses: Genesis 1:27-28, 2:18-25; Matthew 19:4-6; Ephesians 5:20-33.

Scriptural Origins of the Rosary

The Rosary is a traditional and popular devotion that consists of a set of beautiful prayers recited aloud while holding a rosary: a set of beads used to keep track of each prayer. The Rosary begins with the Sign of the Cross and the Apostles' Creed, followed by the prayers of the Our Father, the Hail Mary, and the Glory Be. (Other prayers are sometimes added.) While praying each decade of Hail Marys, one should meditate upon each mystery. The mysteries are biblical events from the lives of Jesus and Mary.

Sign of the Cross (Matthew 28:19)

In the name of the Father, and of the Son, and of the Holy Spirit. Amen.

Our Father (Matthew 6:9-13)

Our Father, who art in heaven, hallowed be thy name; thy kingdom come, thy will be done, on earth as it is in heaven. Give us this day our daily bread, and forgive us our trespasses as we forgive those who trespass against us; and lead us not into temptation, but deliver us from evil. Amen.

Hail Mary

Hail Mary, full of grace, the Lord is with you. (Luke 1:28)

Blessed are you among women, and blessed is the fruit of your womb, Jesus. (Luke 1:42)

Holy Mary, Mother of God, pray for us sinners, now and at the hour of our death. Amen.

Mysteries of the Rosary

Joyful Mysteries (*Storybook* Chapter Eighteen)

The Annunciation (Luke 1:28)

The Visitation (Luke 1:41-42)

The Birth of Christ (Luke 2:7)

The Presentation of Jesus (Luke 2:22-23)

The Finding of the Child Jesus in the Temple (Luke 2:48)

Luminous Mysteries (*Storybook* Chapters Eighteen and Twenty)

The Baptism of Jesus (Luke 3:22)

The Wedding at Cana (John 2:1-11)

The Proclamation of the Kingdom (Matthew 5:1-12)

The Transfiguration (Luke 9:28-36)

The Institution of the Eucharist (Luke 22:19-20)

Sorrowful Mysteries (*Storybook* Chapter Twenty)

The Agony in the Garden (Luke 22:44-45)

The Scourging at the Pillar (John 19:1)

The Crowning with Thorns (Matthew 27:28-29)

Jesus Carries the Cross (John 19:17)

The Crucifixion (Luke 23:46)

Glorious Mysteries
(*Storybook* Chapters Twenty, Twenty-One,
Twenty-Three, and Twenty-Four)

The Resurrection of Christ (Luke 24:1-7)

The Ascension (Luke 24:51)

The Descent of the Holy Spirit (Acts 2:4)

The Assumption of Mary into Heaven (CCC 966)

The Coronation of Mary (Revelation 12:1)

Scripture Quotes Used in Mass Responses

Penitential Act:

Mass Response: "Lord have mercy. Christ have mercy. Lord have mercy." (Found in Chapter Nineteen)

Scripture Quote: "Lord have mercy on us, Son of David" (Matthew 20:31).

Gloria:

Mass Response: "Glory to God in the highest, and on earth peace to people of good will." (Found in Chapter Eighteen)

Scripture Quote: "Glory to God in the highest, and on earth peace among men with whom he is pleased" (Luke 2:14).

Liturgy of the Word:

First Reading: from the Old Testament (Easter Season is from the book of Acts)

Responsorial Psalm: from the book of Psalms

Second Reading: from the New Testament other than the Gospels

The Gospel: from Matthew, Mark, Luke, or John

Eucharistic Prayer:

Mass Response: "Holy, Holy, Holy Lord God of hosts. Heaven and earth are full of your glory. Hosanna in the highest. Blessed is he who comes in the name of the Lord. Hosanna in the highest." (Found in Chapter Twenty)

Scripture Quote: "Holy, holy, holy is the LORD of hosts; the whole earth is full of his glory" (Isaiah 6:3). "Blessed is he who comes in the name of the Lord! Hosanna in the highest!" (Matthew 21:9; Luke 19:38).

Memorial Acclamation:

Mass Response: *"When we eat this Bread and drink this Cup, we proclaim your Death, O Lord, until you come in glory."*

Scripture Quote: *"For as often as you eat this bread and drink the cup, you proclaim the Lord's death until he comes"* (1 Corinthians 11:26).

Mass Response: *"Amen." At the end of the Eucharistic prayer, we respond with the Great Amen.*

Scripture Quote: *"Amen." Amen is used many times in the Bible and is the very last word at the end of the book of Revelation.*

The Communion Rite:

Mass Response and Scripture Quote: *the Our Father* (Matthew 6:9-13; found in Chapter Nineteen).

Sign of Peace:

Mass Response and Scripture Quote: *"Peace be with you"* (John 20:19, 21; found in Chapter Twenty).

Reception of Communion:

Mass Response: *"Lord, I am not worthy that you should enter under my roof; but only say the word, and my soul shall be healed."* (Found in Chapter Eighteen)

Scripture Quote: *"Lord, I am not worthy to have you come under my roof; but only say the word, and my servant will be healed"* (Matthew 8:8).

Directory of the Apostles and Their Ministries

Name	Alternate Names/ Titles	Traditional Place of Death	Author of:
Simon Peter	Cephas (Peter, "Rock"), son of John, son of Jonah	Martyred at Rome; buried beneath St. Peter's Basilica	1 & 2 Peter
Andrew	Brother of Peter	Martyred at Patras	————
James	Son of Zebedee, son of thunder, Boanerges, James the Greater, bishop of Jerusalem	Martyred at Jerusalem	James
John	Son of Zebedee, son of thunder, Boanerges, brother of James, the Beloved Disciple, the Evangelist	Exiled on island of Patmos; died in Ephesus	Gospel of John; 1, 2, 3 John; Revelation
Philip	from Bethsaida	Martyred at Hierapolis	————
Bartholomew	Nathaniel, son of Tomay, of Cana in Galilee	Martyred at Armenia	————
Thomas	Doubting Thomas, Didymus, the Twin	Martyred at India	————

Name	Alternate Names/ Titles	Traditional Place of Death	Author of:
Matthew	The tax collector, Levi, the son of Alphaeus, the Evangelist	Martyred at Ethiopia	Gospel of Matthew
James (the son of Alphaeus)	James the Less	Martyred at Ostrakine	——————
Simon (who was called the Zealot)	Simon the Cananaean	Martyred at Persia	——————
Judas (the son of James)	Thaddeus, Judas not Iscariot	Martyred at Persia	——————
Judas Iscariot who became a traitor	Son of Perdition	Jerusalem; buried in Potter's Field	——————
Others mentioned in Bible:			
Matthias	Replacement for Judas Iscariot		
Paul	Saul	Martyred at Rome	Romans; 1, 2 Corinthians; Galatians; Ephesians; Philippians; Colossians; 1, 2 Thessalonians; 1, 2 Timothy; Titus; Philemon; Hebrews
Luke	The Evangelist, the Physician	Greece	Gospel of Luke; Acts
Mark	John Mark, the Evangelist	Martyred at Alexandria	Gospel of Mark

About the Authors

Emily Cavins

Emily has assisted her husband, Jeff, in the development of *The Bible Timeline: The Story of Salvation*. She is the author of *My Heart Is a Violin* and *Lily of the Mohawks: The Story of St. Kateri*. Emily is also the writer of "Family Night," a weekly column based on the current Sunday Mass readings. She received her degree in classical and Near-Eastern archaeology from the University of Minnesota. Jeff and Emily have three daughters.

Lisa Bromschwig

Lisa is a convert to Catholicism and has a passion for Jesus in the Word and sacraments. She has a master's degree in pastoral ministry from St. Paul Seminary in St. Paul, Minnesota, and works as a director of religious education at a large suburban parish. She has served as a catechist in Catholic religious education programs and a substitute teacher in Catholic schools. Lisa and her husband, Kurt, have three children.

Regina Lickteig Neville

Regina received her bachelor's degree in education and theatre liberal arts from the University of Northern Iowa and a master of fine arts degree from Yale University. She has spent over a decade managing non-profit theatre companies in Chapel Hill, North Carolina, and in the San Francisco Bay area. Regina also holds a Minnesota teaching license, has worked as a director of religious education, and has taught faith formation for more than fifteen years. She serves in leadership roles in education and with her church community. Regina and her husband, Tom, have three children.

Linda Wandrei

Linda is a full-time wife and mother. She received her bachelor's degree in business administration from the University of St. Thomas, St. Paul, Minnesota. She has catechized children from pre-school to sixth grade in local parishes and vacation Bible school programs for the past fifteen years. She also served as a Bible study coordinator for Jeff Cavins' *Great Adventure* series "Adventures in the Acts of the Apostles," with 450 participants. Linda was raised Catholic and was inspired to teach her children the fullness of truth and love upon which the Catholic Church is built. Motivated by that same love, she feels a great desire to see a Catholic Bible study for children come to fruition. She and her husband, Phil, have three children.

Ascension Press is excited to partner with **Gen2Rev® Catholic Bible Studies, LLC** to publish *The Great Adventure Storybook*. This narrative of the Catholic Bible aligns with *The Great Adventure Bible Timeline* to bring children and adults together as they learn God's Word. Gen2Rev® Catholic Bible Studies, LLC offers additional support materials to the *Storybook,* including:

- *The Gen2Rev® Beginners' Guidebook* for grades K-2

- *The Gen2Rev® Intermediate Guidebook* for grades 3-5

- *The Gen2Rev® Advanced Guidebook* for grades 6 and up

- *Gen2Rev® Plays* that dramatize each chapter of the *Storybook*

More information on these other resources can be found at Gen2Revcatholic.com.